MISSION ACCOMPLISHED

By the same author

A Man With a Mission, Book Guild Publishing, 2009

MISSION ACCOMPLISHED

Canon John Taylor, OBE

Book Guild Publishing

Sussex, England

First published in Great Britain in 2015 by
The Book Guild Ltd
The Werks
45 Church Road
Brighton, BN3 2BE

Typesetting in Times by
Keyboard Services, Luton, Bedfordshire

Printed and bound in Great Britain by
CPI Group (UK) Ltd, Croydon, CR0 4YY

A catalogue record for this book is available from
The British Library.

ISBN 978 1 910508 01 5

Contents

Foreword

I first met Canon John, in any meaningful way, at the formal opening, by Princess Alexandra, of the new nursing homes at St George's Park. I remember being impressed at how at ease he had seemed with her, impressed because I am a transplanted American, for whom such things were unknown and quite intimidating. I was even more impressed when he subsequently made a point of coming to speak to me. It was the first of what has turned out very happily to be many conversations, each incredibly interesting, like the man himself. I got to know him even better through his kind gift of his first book, *A Man With a Mission*, and am truly delighted that he is bringing his story up to date with *Mission Accomplished*, though it is my fervent hope that it is far from accomplished yet.

He has led a life of great adventure in the service of the Lord, which is of course the greatest adventure of all, and that is exactly how he has seen it. He has worked with some of the most needy in our world, but mixes well with every sort of person, in every sort of place, all of whom he sees as God's children. He speaks of his 'retirement' at St George's Park, but I hope it is entirely clear that 'retirement' is a relative word, and his ministry to the St George's village community, and to the residents (180 of them) at the three nursing homes, is both demanding and essential.

His whole life has been one of service, and 'denomination' has always played only a secondary part of that: he lives our Lord's prayer 'that they might all be one,' and I personally am a great beneficiary of that. The Sisters at St George's are delighted with his ministry there, as has been the Bishop of the Catholic Diocese of Arundel and Brighton, and he has become a good friend to all the Sisters, and to me. He is a living example of the ecumenism that is the true hope for unity among Christians in these troubled times.

I can heartily recommend *Mission Accomplished* and strongly advise reading *A Man With a Mission* first. And as for Canon John and his life and word, I can only pray '*ad multos annos*'.

Father Rick McGrath
Parish Priest, St Wilfrid's Catholic Church, Burgess Hill

Preface

Since the launch of my autobiography, *A Man with a Mission*, in September 2009, covering my ministry up to when I left Thailand in 1981, I have been put under considerable pressure to update it. But publishing is an expensive undertaking. I have been reliably told that 85% of books published result in a financial loss. Mine is no exception. It would have been good just to recover the outlay, but money was not the objective. Rather it was to record an account of God's blessing on my ministry, not only in congregational worship but also to prisoners, refugees and drug addicts, and patients in hospitals and hospices, to name but a few; to show that the love and compassion of Almighty God extends to every corner of His universe, to saint and sinner alike – and that includes me.

Finances apart, there are other considerations to take into account. I am now eighty-six years of age and have, for the last eight years, been receiving treatment for prostate cancer. Thanks to the dedication of the staff of the National Health Service, I am doing extremely well; although, as one medic cheerfully told me, 'It will get you in the end!'

There is no doubt that my ministry up to the point of leaving Thailand was far more colourful than what followed. So would an account of my Chaplaincy in Rotterdam, my appointment as Vicar of Warnham and then being licensed as priest in charge of Streat and Westmeston in Sussex be an anti-climax or not? In one sense, it wouldn't. I have always said that promotion in the church is being where God wants you to be. I believe that this is what happened to me and although my ministry has not been as exotic since Thailand, I do believe it has been equally blessed. Updating my ministry will, I trust, make that abundantly clear and will undoubtedly be of interest to my family and others who have asked me to complete it.

So what to do? I have decided to complete my autobiography and paint a broad picture of the time that followed, supplemented by events that illustrate specific aspects of my ministry. But even as I contemplate it I can see there will be a different emphasis. My ministry up to leaving Thailand was mainly centred on people, either as individuals or groups, whereas what followed, especially in Rotterdam, was rather about properties, mission buildings and finances – a ministry of management rather than of pastoring. There is one final point I need to make. Both books are focused on my ministry and I have only referred to my private life as and when it has directly impinged upon my vocation. After the death of Rose, I journeyed through some very turbulent waters, including two unhappy personal relationships. For this reason I am not going to dwell on them, except to say that at no time was my faith affected; through all the trials and tribulations of those difficult times I received unqualified support from my bishops and church officers who encouraged me to continue where I was in my ministry. But, praise the Lord, after the storm came the calm and with it my marriage to Millie, which has been richly blessed. It is thanks to her that I feel able to complete the record of my ministry.

I dedicated *A Man with a Mission* to Rose. What follows I dedicate to Millie.

Introduction

The end of *A Man with a Mission* documented my retreat to The Franciscan House at Falmouth in 1981, where I went to seek God's will for my future ministry. After the death of Rose, I just knew I couldn't continue in Thailand; her death reawakened in me a nagging urge to become a Franciscan monk. I had for a long time considered being a lay member of the order, but being chaplain to the British Embassy, and ministering to a largely expatriate community, wouldn't allow me to live the simple life that was required. The death of Rose changed all that. I had already decided to move on from Thailand; was God now calling me to be a monk? I needed time to decide my future and whether to embark upon what was clearly an unpopular proposition to those who knew me; after a week of consideration, I will never forget the look of relief on my friends' faces as they greeted me outside the retreat house, knowing now that God had clearly shown me that I was not destined to be a monk.

One of my favourite sayings is, 'If God doesn't come, He sends!' My retreat did not reveal His answer through fasting, silence, prayers, meditation, and worship, but through a lady golfer! (For details, please read the last chapter of *A Man with a Mission*.) As my friends drove me back to their house in Shap Wells, I tried to take in the implications of this revelation and to wonder what form my future ministry would take.

As recorded in *A Man with a Mission*, I made a vow at my ordination that I would never apply for a job, but wait to be invited, and the death of Rose in no way altered that resolution. However, unless others were aware that my Thai ministry was drawing to a close, no invitations would be forthcoming. I began to build the necessary awareness by first informing my family and friends of my decision. Like many expatriates, I used to send a round robin to my friends once or twice a year. Because of the nature of my diverse ministry, copies winged their way literally all over the world, with a mailing list of over 250. My status as embassy chaplain at Bangkok allowed me to use forces mail, but once that ceased I knew (because of the expense of postage) that my future list would have to be seriously curtailed. But this was news that I wanted to share with everyone, so to heck with the cost; everyone got a copy.

By return of post came the replies, expressing delight (and relief!) at my decision not to become a monk. Also included were suggestions not only regarding how I should tackle my future, but in what direction I should move. The Missions to Seamen (now Mission to Seafarers), whom I had served as a lay reader at the beginning of my ministry, wrote shortly after my ordination that 'they had their beady eyes on me'. They now wrote along similar lines, offering me the appointment as senior chaplain to Rotterdam, then the largest port in the world. Being chaplain included appointment as the society's secretary to the Netherlands. Although Rotterdam seemed to be a possible choice, I had very serious reservations about accepting it because of an increasing desire for parish ministry. The various aspects of seafarers' work involved a great deal of practical ministry, which took up much precious time. When, however, I was told that the senior chaplain of Rotterdam was also the chaplain to St Mary's (the Anglican Church in Rotterdam), that argument was somewhat diminished. Also Prebendary Arthur Royall, the Church of England clergy appointment officer at that time, whose task was to help clergy who wanted to move parishes or were returning to the UK from overseas postings, was not hopeful that he could find me a suitable living because of the length of time I had been away from the UK. He knew of the Missions to Seamen's offer and urged me to take it.

In the meantime I had put a notice in the *Church Times* explaining my position and was agreeably surprised, despite the appointments officer's pessimism, to receive offers to visit five vacant incumbencies in and around the UK and Wales. So I bought an old banger and spent the next six weeks travelling around the country looking at the various positions offered. Whether there was a shortage of clergymen I do not know, but in every case I was offered the living. Sadly I didn't feel that any of them pressed the right buttons. One rural dean, for example, said to me of a certain parish that I visited, 'This is ideal for you as a refugee family has just moved in!' As I had been used to dealing with thousands of refugees in Thailand, I was not particularly impressed. The main problem with them all, however, was that after ministering in three countries – Thailand, Vietnam and Laos – the thought of my work being confined to a comparatively small area was claustrophobic. Furthermore, in Thailand I had a ministry to hospitals, detention centres, prisons, refugee camps, work with the Samaritans, marriage guidance and AA, plus setting up ministries in three different parts of the country, to say nothing of ecumenical activity. To accept a Parish with only one hospital or prison within its boundaries (or even none), plus the fact that on more than one occasion I was told, 'This side of the road will be yours, but the other side belongs to the next parish and is out of bounds,' proved to be the straw that broke the camel's back.

As I viewed my options, Rotterdam opened out in front of me, offering so much more scope, space and opportunity for various aspects of ministry than anywhere in England. Consequently, it was there that I finally decided to go. I was appointed on a five-year contract, but actually stayed for six.

Rotterdam (1983–1990)

Little did I realise what a can of worms was waiting to be opened up. The then-present incumbent was supposed to have been a temporary appointment. Previous to him, the senior chaplain had developed a brain tumour and subsequently died. Considering the size and importance of Rotterdam, an immediate replacement was required. I was given an insight into what a rough ride ahead I might receive when I learned that, as the senior chaplain's tumour developed, some of his actions became odd, to say the least! But instead of sympathetically wondering why, a black book was opened up by some senior members of the congregation, recording any strange actions to be reported to higher authorities. Thank goodness, as far as I am aware, no black book was ever started about me. However much St Mary's PCC sometimes took an odd line from my viewpoint, usually our views were in harmony.

As already mentioned, when the previous senior chaplain suddenly died, the society couldn't leave the position unattended because of the station's importance, so an assistant chaplain from a Belgian port was transferred to Rotterdam. It was explained to him that this was a temporary move until a permanent successor could be found, but this took time. A good few years elapsed before I arrived on the scene and in the meantime, the temporary chaplain had, to all intents and purposes, become a permanent fixture. That situation might have continued indefinitely, but there was a problem; whereas his pastoral gifts were exceptional, those of administration left much to be desired. Being secretary for the Netherlands, chaplain to St Mary's Anglican Church, running the main mission in the centre of Rotterdam, having oversight of two more missions in Schiedam and Pernis, including the staff who ran them, to say nothing of being responsible for up to four UK students in the team, plus a secretary and a bookkeeper, was just too much. Chaos reigned. I don't believe a black book was started in his case, but I do know that head office received many complaints about his organisational abilities, which is how I came into the picture. There were many decisions which urgently needed to be made, but in fact no new initiatives had been undertaken during his tenancy, so

1

problems increased through inaction. As a result, the financial position was dire and the smooth running of the stations left much to be desired. For example, in the early days, the three mission stations all had souvenir shops, which provided income. A bookkeeper was appointed for all three, keeping the stock at the Rotterdam Mission. But as I soon found out, there was no longer a shop at Pieter de Hochberg and very little business taking place in the other two; the bookkeeper had been unnecessarily employed for the last ten years!

There was also a huge problem with the chaplain's secretary. The first time I tried to dictate some letters, I discovered that she was incapable of receiving either dictation or typing. She came from one of the leading families in St Mary's congregation, but unfortunately had a severe drinking problem. My predecessor thought that giving her a job would help her overcome her problem. Experience proved him wrong. By giving her dictation first thing in the morning, she could just about get by, but by 11.00 a.m. she was incapable of anything. One of my first priorities therefore was to terminate hers and the bookkeeper's contracts, but this was easier said than done! Because of her family's important status in St Mary's congregation, I had to move extremely carefully. There were also laws regarding termination of employment, which included considerable compensation. As a consequence, I was making myself unpopular, but it did mean a reduction of salaries and it set in motion the long road to financial recovery.

This highlighted the biggest problem of all – the whole complex of the Missions to Seamen in Holland was fast approaching bankruptcy. But there was more; the main mission in Rotterdam was now in the wrong place and obviously needed to be closed. It was built at a time when most of the ships berthed on the River Maas, so with the mission sited on the river bank it was in the ideal place. But that was now history. Huge areas of land around the estuary of the mass had been reclaimed and a new container port had been constructed. These were at least 15 miles from the mission at Pieter de Hochberg, rendering it surplus to requirement.

As Rotterdam was the largest port in the world, there were other seamen's societies working there and all had basically the same problem as we did – being in the wrong place due to the port's development. Furthermore, despite the number of societies for serving seamen, there were ships that remained unvisited. Conversely, others had more than one society on board. Sometimes it seemed we were working in opposition rather than harmonising with one another! The picture below shows the number of other societies working in the port. In planning our future, I obviously needed to take into account the work of other societies, to avoid duplication and complications! I increasingly came to the conclusion that one all-embracing building, which could be used by all seamen's societies, centred near the heart of the new port complex, was the way forward. This, in due time, came to pass and proved to be a great success.

SEAMEN'S SOCIETIES

A THE MISSIONS TO SEAMEN - 'DE BEER'
01819 - 6 23 77 ⊞ (A) ⚓ ♪ ○ ⑤

B NORWEGIAN KONG OLAVS KAPELL
01819 - 6 22 09 and 6 22 63 ⊞ (L) ⌴ ○ ⑤

C INTERNATIONAL SEAMEN'S CENTRE 'DE BEER'
01819 - 6 23 77 ☐ ✕ 🛏 ⌴ ⚓ ○ ⑤ ♪ ⊐

C MUNICIPAL OFFICE SEAMEN'S WELFARE, Branch office 'De Beer'
01819 - 6 35 68 ☐

D THE MISSIONS TO SEAMEN - PERNIS
010 - 16 27 80 ⊞ (A) ⚓ ♪ ⑤ ○

G NORWEGIAN SPORTS GROUND 'NORGE'
010 - 29 20 68 and 29 74 73 ☐ ✕ ○

H DANISH SEAMEN'S CHURCH
010 - 76 40 16 ⊞ (L) ○ ⑤

I THE MISSIONS TO SEAMEN - ROTTERDAM
010 - 76 40 43 ⊞ (A) ⚓ ♪ ⑤ ○

J SEAMEN'S SPORT CENTRE
010 - 29 07 02 and 13 39 99 ☐ ⚓ ○

K FINNISH SEAMEN'S CHURCH
010 - 36 61 64 ⊞ (L) ⌴ ○ ⑤

L NORWEGIAN SEAMEN'S CHURCH
010 - 36 57 23 ⊞ (L) ⌴ ⑤

M GERMAN SEAMEN's HOME
010 - 36 39 36 and 36 56 05 ⊞ (L) 🛏 ⚓ ✕ ♪ ○ ⑤

N SWEDISH SEAMEN'S CHURCH
010 - 36 54 61 ⊞ (L) ⌴ ○ ⑤ ⊐

O SEAMEN'S CLUB ROTTERDAM
010 - 36 67 83, 36 17 28, 11 92 60 ☐ ⊞ (DR) 🛏 ✕ ⌴ ♪ ⑤

P MUNINIPAL OFFICE 'SEAMEN'S WELFARE'
010 - 13 39 99 and 17 29 69 ☐

S GERMAN SEAMEN'S HOME, Branch office 'De Beer'
01819 - 6 23 77

⊞ A Christian centre of chaplaincy (followed by abbreviated denomination/s in brackets)
☐ A centre not specifically Christian
✕ Meals
🛏 Beds
⌴ Snacks
⚓ Bar
○ Football
⑤ Shop
⊐ Swimming pool
♪ Dancing

The Seamen's Societies in Rotterdam.

REBUILDING THE ROTTERDAM COMPLEX

It was decided that the clubs at Perlis and Schiedam, having no other missions in the area, should remain. But in closing down our main mission at Pieter de Hochberg, very careful planning was necessary.

3

When the mission was built it was decided that the Anglican Church of St Mary's would be built on a small plot of land adjacent to it. Unfortunately the plot was only large enough to accommodate the main body of the church, which meant that there was no room for the vestry, or office space and a meeting room. It was decided to build these facilities on the mission plot, which at the time seemed a reasonable idea – the Missions to Seamen chaplain also being the chaplain of St Mary's. But what if church and mission needed to be separated? The break up could be catastrophic for St Mary's church. In my briefing at head office I was made aware of some of these problems, but no solution was offered. 'You can sort it all out once you get there,' I was airily informed.

As it turned out, I was given plenty of time to think about it as yet another problem arose – the relocation of the present chaplain. Head office had intended to post him to an English mission, but he was married to a Dutch lady who refused point blank to move to England. Furthermore, she was incensed that (in her eyes) her husband was being unfairly removed and denied that he was ever told that his was a temporary appointment. For this reason she declined at first to move out of the mission house. Shortly before I arrived, she had forcibly made her views known during a church service, which immediately divided the congregation between those who sympathised with her and those who didn't.

A clue to the fact that his was a temporary appointment was to be seen in the house in which he and his family had stayed and into which I was destined to move. It had originally been bought for one of the assistant chaplains, but was totally inadequate for a senior chaplain. Why? Because there was no study; so one of the bedrooms upstairs had been utilised for this purpose. This meant that if anyone called to see the chaplain the whole house would be opened up, providing no privacy for the chaplain's family. I could just imagine poor mother trying to put the children to bed, at the same time as a visitor was tramping up the stairs, full of his own problems! But, in any case, the fact that she would not move out meant there was no house for me to move into! This proved to be a blessing in disguise because, realising that the house was totally inadequate for the senior chaplain, I made clear to head office that I needed a house with a study. I firmly rejected head office's suggestions that I should move into the present house and then sort it out. A further problem arose, which meant I couldn't move in anyway. When after negotiations she finally agreed to move her family to another house in the Netherlands, there was a caveat; the children had just started a new term at school and she wouldn't allow them to be moved until the term was over. I had some sympathy with her, so agreed that they could stay in the house until the end of term. All things considered, this proved to be a blessing. It gave me a chance to become more knowledgeable about the past and to get a better grasp of the present. It also gave me the opportunity to get to know the port committee, St Mary's PCC and the mission staff, and to familiarise myself with routine matters.

My first meeting with the port committee proved to be a nightmare! There was only one item on the agenda. Because the Rotterdam Missions to Seamen was bankrupt, it should be closed down!

I rose to my feet and began my maiden speech. 'Gentlemen,' I said, 'I am perfectly capable of conducting a funeral on my own; I do not need a committee to assist me. But I do need one to help me turn things around and that's what I'm asking from you today.'

The trouble with port committees, unlike PCCs (the parish equivalent), is that almost without exception they are business men and not necessarily religiously inclined. As a consequence, the spiritual aspect of the work was very much secondary to its financial credibility. To my profound relief, however, they agreed to a stay of execution.

'We will review the situation in a year's time,' they told me. Thus ended my first meeting, but not the end of my immediate problems. As already mentioned, there were, at any one time, four student helpers on the Rotterdam staff. They came from a mixture of backgrounds; some were taking a year off from academic studies before going on to university; others had been before an ordination selection committee and while not rejected outright, were told to go out there and get some experience of life before applying again; others, who were at the crossroads of life, were not sure which way they should go and were seeking some direction through their time in Rotterdam. But the experience to which they were being subjected was not the sort the examining boards had in mind, nor did it help them to sort out their futures!

I had been told that their accommodation left a lot to be desired, so after my first fateful meeting with the port committee, I went to visit them in their flat. I was immediately unimpressed by the area. To put it mildly, it was run down and tacky. I found their flat number and entered the block wherein it was housed. I was greeted by the barking of a ferocious dog, chained to the stair rail and partly blocking my entrance to the flats above. The barking continued for a few moments until the ground-floor door opened to reveal a lady who could be none other than a prostitute. If there was any doubt about her profession it was immediately quashed by her opening words and invitation, which left nothing to the imagination. As any who have read my first book will know, I had experienced something similar in Tiger Bay, Cardiff at the beginning of my ministry.

I hastily made my excuses and, making myself as slim possible, squeezed past the ferocious dog and ascended the stairs. Goodness knows how many steps later I finally reached my destination. I rang the bell to be warmly welcomed by the students. Their accommodation, however, left me in no doubt that as a matter of urgency they needed to be moved elsewhere. This I promised I would effect as soon as possible. I was dreading my downstairs journey, which luckily proved uneventful, because, I assumed, the dog and the ladies were otherwise engaged.

The first time I boarded a plane to investigate my appointment at Rotterdam, my mind was full of unanswered questions. As I surrendered my return ticket and sank thankfully into my seat for the short journey home, I felt overwhelmed with what I had discovered and the magnitude of the task ahead. Then I recalled some wise words from a daily prayer I use: 'Help us to become more like your Son Jesus Christ, so that your power may be revealed in our weakness.' And in any case, 'It's God's Church and not mine!' So I offered up these thoughts in prayer, ending with 'Into thy hands O Lord I commend my spirit' and then fell asleep.

WAITING TO MOVE

Apart from trying to absorb the magnitude of the complexities and challenges awaiting me at Rotterdam, I also had to overcome some enormous personal and emotional obstacles before I would be ready to embark on a new way of life. I was now on my own after almost thirty years of happily married life with Rose. We married in 1952 and shortly afterwards set sail 'on a slow boat to China', as the popular song at that time recorded. Destination: Hong Kong. So began an expatriate lifestyle, which is entirely different from anything in the

UK. Three years in Hong Kong, two years at St Michael's Theological College, two years in Wales, twelve years in Tanzania and then eight in Thailand gobbled up some twenty-seven years. Apart from anything else, expatriate life also included servants! True, there was a two-year gap without them after ordination and before we moved to Tanganyika, but a loving wife meant that yet again I could concentrate on my ministry, rather than on household chores. To my shame, I must admit (in common, I suspect, with many fathers of that era) I cannot recall changing a single nappy for either Michael or Elizabeth! No wonder then that taking up the British way of life once again in 1982, and alone, I found very challenging, particularly cooking and the household chores. Ready prepared meals soon palled and, to make matters worse, I found going to restaurants on my own very depressing, to say nothing of the cost.

To fill in the three-month gap before moving to Rotterdam, I was sent to 'caretake' the mission in Middlesbrough, a club known as a 'home mission'. The mission and the chaplain's house were combined into one unit, the mission being on the ground floor and the chaplain's accommodation above but with a shared kitchen on the ground floor. The concept was to provide 'a home from home' for visiting seafarers. The chaplain and his wife, around whom the concept was planned, were very enthusiastic and the system worked very well for them, especially as she loved cooking and entertaining! But when they moved on there was no suitable successor, so the mission became 'mothballed', pending a decision on its future, hence my being there for three months. Living in a huge complex in its own grounds (I was going to 'say miles from anywhere', which is not quite true, but certainly without neighbours), I found terribly lonely and utterly depressing. Also, if I am honest, boring! On the other hand, when I contemplated Rotterdam and the amount of energy and time that would be needed to turn it around, I began to wonder if I would ever find time to manage the house I was to live in. One thing was certain, however, and that was that I wouldn't have time to properly clean or prepare meals. So I hit on the bright idea of employing a housekeeper.

THE RISE AND FALL OF HOUSEKEEPER MO

Enquiries revealed that there was a magazine called *The Lady* that dealt with such matters, so without further ado I sent them a letter explaining my position and enclosing a suggested advert. I was amazed to receive their reply. It told me that advertising to take a lady out of the country was not allowed as it could be construed as soliciting! They couldn't therefore print my advert. I was advised instead to study their magazine, as there were always housekeepers applying for positions, and to make contact with one who might seem suitable.

The local newsagent provided the latest issue, which I eagerly scanned to find the relevant section, headed, I seem to remember, 'Domestic help'. In it were about eight ladies seeking new positions but whose details, to my uneducated mind, seemed inseparable in content. To complicate matters, I was due to fly to Rotterdam the following morning, so I decided to rush off an identical letter to them all. This I did and then promptly put the matter out of mind. Time was of the essence as I had to be back in Middlesbrough by the Saturday to prepare for an 8.00 a.m. communion with sermon on the Sunday morning. (I was helping out in the local church, St Cuthbert's, who were at that time without an incumbent.)

On the Rotterdam agenda were meetings with the staff at the various missions, the PCC and port committee, plus looking at four possible houses for the senior chaplain's residence, as well as finding more suitable accommodation for the students. My feet, to quote a popular expression, didn't touch the ground and as a consequence, by the time I arrived back in the Middlesbrough mission about 5.30 p.m. on the Saturday, I was totally exhausted.

The first thing that caught my eye as I unlocked the front door was the amount of mail lying on the mat. I retired to my office to check that there was nothing requiring my immediate attention. I was relieved to find that no one had died, been taken to hospital, or was in need of counselling. I also found that there were half a dozen letters from potential housekeepers who had responded to my letter. These I put to one side to concentrate on my top priority, which was to prepare my sermon for the following morning.

I had barely put pen to paper when the strident tones of the telephone forced me to pick it up, but with my mind still firmly centred on finishing my sermon I said, almost automatically, 'Canon John, can I help you?'

Back came the reply, 'This is Mo.'

'Mo?' I replied. 'I don't know any Mos. You must have the wrong number.'

To which, in an obviously hurt tone, the caller replied, 'But haven't you read my letter?'

I tried to explain that I had just returned from Rotterdam so hadn't had chance to read any mail!

She replied, 'Well please have a look; you will know mine as I have enclosed a photograph.'

Telling her to hang on a minute, I browsed quickly through the pile of letters on my desk and sure enough out fell a photo of a lady, whom I presumed was Mo. I started to explain that because of other pressing matters I wouldn't be able to cope with my mail until Monday morning when I was cut off in mid-sentence. For those who know me that is saying something!

'But I'm actually on my way to you right now!' she told me. Without seemingly even pausing to draw breath, she continued to tell me that the Lord had told her that her mission in life from now on was looking after me. As a consequence she had handed in her notice to the hotel where she was working so that she would be immediately available to start work. There was more; so certain was she that the Lord wanted her to spend the rest of her life looking after me, she was phoning from a phone box about 16 miles from where I sat, so would be with me shortly! Mesmerised by this incredible turn of events and wondering what on earth I had let myself in for, I attempted to stop her flow but failed miserably. So, only half-listening to what she was saying, I tried to rationalise the situation. True, I had written to her and she was, after all, replying in an extremely positive manner (if somewhat over the top). If I were to appoint her (or another applicant) she would have to live in, so staying the night would be the norm if she was appointed. I also realised that I had to be very careful; otherwise the situation could get completely out of hand.

By now feeling more in charge, I firmly cut short her ramblings, which I noticed had by now moved on to telling me in intimate detail why she had divorced her husband, and laid down the conditions under which she could stay the night. As she had signed out of her hotel and was on her way to me, I told her she could stay the night, but I couldn't see her in the morning as I had an early communion service. She had to be gone by the time I returned from the first service, as I had people coming to see me who would demand my undivided attention. I would contact her in due course, but in the meantime I had to return to Holland for further meetings, so she needed to be patient. I also pointed out that having just returned from abroad I had no food in the house, so couldn't feed her. Finally I told her that I was only caretaking the house, that it was only partly furnished, but there were five bedrooms, one of which I would get ready for her. To

9

all this she agreed and rang off. I hastily made sure that a bedroom was prepared and then returned to my study to continue my sermon preparation. Because of its urgency I became completely engrossed, until I was startled by the loud roar of a car that screamed to a halt just outside the study window. Looking out I saw a red MG sports model, complete with open top. Out jumped a blonde lady nursing what proved to be a bottle of wine and advanced purposefully towards the front door. I took a moment to check from the photo that it was indeed Mo, whom I noticed seemed somewhat older than an MG and blonde hair would seem to suggest, and answered the door.

'Hi,' she said rather unnecessarily. 'It's me: Mo.'

'And I'm Canon John,' I replied in as authoritative a tone as I could. The effect of this was somewhat muted, however, when she thrust the bottle of wine into my hands.

'Have you eaten?' was her next question, which I assumed was her housekeeper training. When I replied in the negative, she suggested that we nipped down to town to get a Chinese takeaway. Up to this moment I had decided to forgo an evening meal, but the word Chinese brought back memories of eating in Hong Kong and Thailand and suddenly I was very hungry.

I must divert from the narrative to tell you that the old banger that I had purchased to visit the parishes had packed in and was in the local garage being repaired. To keep me mobile they kindly loaned me an old white van, the only problem being that it had once belonged to a fishmonger and its powerful stench of stale fish remained! This proved to be no problem to Mo, who volunteered to drive me down to town in her MG. So, a few minutes later, with me holding onto my seat like grim death, we roared off and soon, with a screeching of brakes, pulled up outside a Chinese takeaway. In no time at all we were back at the mission. I had explained about the unfinished sermon, so she suggested that I completed it while she got the meal ready in the kitchen. To this I happily and gratefully agreed.

About ten minutes later she came to the study and told me, 'Supper is served.' I walked into the kitchen but couldn't believe my eyes! Instead of the rather harsh neon lights that I had become used to, the room was lit by about six candles strategically placed around the room and on the table. Serviettes, folded to represent lotus flowers, were in abundance. And from somewhere (I presume the garden), the centre of the table boasted an expertly arranged vase of flowers. A bottle of wine and glasses completed the transformation! During supper I endeavoured to enlighten her about the situation in Holland and what I was expecting from her. No matter what I said, she agreed, repeating on more than one occasion that the Lord had told her the only reason she had been put on earth was to look after me! It all seemed too good to be true and I began to panic at what possibly lay ahead.

When the meal was over, she suggested that I went to my study to finish off any work whilst she prepared some coffee. There was a small room upstairs that had been partly furnished, with a couple of armchairs, a small table, plus a television, as well as curtains on the windows, which I had never closed because the window overlooked the football pitch and fields beyond. It was where I retired at the end of the day and was the obvious place to drink our coffees. I thankfully finished off my sermon and wended my way upstairs and into the room. Again I couldn't believe my eyes at the transformation! More candles, curtains drawn, and the two armchairs were now placed side by side, separated only by a small table that housed the coffee cups.

'You do look tired,' were her words of greeting. 'Do come, sit down and relax.' She patted first the arm of my waiting chair, smiling sweetly at me as I advanced, and then patting my arm as I sat down. The only consolation was that the coffee was first class! I attempted to channel the conversation along more business lines, but the ambience and candlelight made the going difficult. Something she then said made me realise that I was now in a very delicate situation, and I offered up a silent prayer for help. Help came, but not in the way I imagined. The piercing sound of the front door bell interrupted the conversation.

'Who could that be at this late hour?' Mo exploded.

I explained that being a priest meant that one's front door bell rang at all sorts of times, that it was probably someone in trouble, and that I would go and see, so please excuse me. As I left the room I heard her say, with what seemed unnecessary venom, 'Just get rid of him!'

Needless to say, getting rid of whoever was knocking on the door was the last thing on my mind! Standing on the doorstep was a rather sad and dejected member of the local congregation, who tearfully told me that he had just had a huge row with his wife and didn't know what to do next.

'Do come in,' I rather too enthusiastically said, which must have seemed to him rather odd, but which immediately solved my problem. I took him to my study, sat him down and explained that I had a visitor upstairs, so I would appreciate it if he could excuse me for a few minutes, while I explained my need to leave her.

Mo was furious and offered various comments and suggestions on how to deal with such an intrusion at that time of night. Needless to say, none of them were suitable, especially for a possible housekeeper to a priest, so she got short thrift from me. I explained that I expected to be down in my study for a long time, so she should retire. I reiterated that I had to be away early in the morning, but that I expected her to be gone by the time I returned, and that in due course she would hear from me. I thanked her for coming and, much relieved, retreated to my study.

In fact the interview did (thankfully) last a long time, before he finally left. After which, dousing the ground-floor lights, I approached the stairs leading to the bedrooms. The first thing I noticed was that there was a light at the top of the stairs, which undoubtedly came from Mo's bedroom. As I climbed the stairs I could see that it was her bedside table lamp strategically placed, so that I couldn't miss its alluring light! But what brought shivers tingling down my spine was the overpowering odour of scent that came wafting down the stairs and engulfed me. To complete the nightmare, I heard the gentle sound of coughing that left me in no doubt that Mo was very much alive!

I stopped in my tracks to consider what to do next. I then resorted to something that I had never ever been reduced to in thirty years of marriage. I took my shoes off and crept up the remaining stairs! Barely daring to breathe, I safely navigated the last few steps and then fled to my bedroom at the far end of the corridor, locking the door safely behind me. Thankfully she was gone by the time I returned from the early service the following morning. But not forgotten! Getting rid of her was one of the hardest tasks I have ever undertaken, which, once and for all, made me vow that – dirty house or not, starving or emaciated, lonely or not – I would never, ever, again attempt to employ a housekeeper! To calm the situation down, I informed Mo and the other ladies who had written to me that I was going to delay making any appointments until after I had arrived and settled down in Rotterdam. This seemed to satisfy the other applicants but not Mo. By almost daily telephone calls, she wanted to know what progress had been made and when did I want her to move in.

THE MOVE TO ROTTERDAM

The three months passed and I finally moved to Rotterdam. I felt a sense of release; there was now all that water separating us! My release was short-lived, however. To greet me on my arrival came a huge plant and an intensity of telephone calls. One of my first tasks was to write to Mo and the other ladies who had applied for the position of housekeeper, explaining that I had now decided against having one, certainly for the time being, and thanking them for their interest. I assured them that if, at a later date, I did decide to go ahead, their application would be amongst the first to be considered. End of story? Not quite. Mo wrote and said that she was coming over to Rotterdam and had indeed booked her passage on the ferry, so would I please meet her? I rang her telling her not to come, that I wouldn't meet or see her and if she still insisted on coming, I would contact the police, complaining of harassment. She replied that she had already paid for her ticket. I offered and indeed sent her a refund of her expenditure and, praise the Lord, that finally put to bed (excuse the pun) the saga of Mo.

In complete contrast to Mo's desire to be with me was the negative reaction to my arrival by the priest from whom I was taking over. Because of the problems over his transfer to a mission in the UK, head office decided that he would stay on, certainly for the time being, as my number two – surely an impossible situation for him, but equally so for me. I had informed him of the details of my arrival and expected him to meet me at the airport. He didn't. After waiting in vain for about half an hour, I took a taxi to the mission, only to find that it was locked up, with no one in sight. I found a phone box and rang his house, to find him in. Under the arrangement I was to inherit his (the senior chaplain's) car, which I asked him to deliver to me at the mission and also to bring me some keys. He duly arrived, opened up the mission and we went together to the office. He then threw the car keys onto the desk, plus a huge bunch of about twenty others, and volunteered the fact that he was now off to pick up his children from school. Trying to keep my cool, I urged him to give me some sort of handover before he left, enlighten me regarding the huge bunch of keys and answer some urgent questions. I acknowledged the fact that it must be extremely difficult for him but that both of us must work together to make the changeover as smooth and stress-free as possible.

Be that as it may, he left some twenty minutes later and there was I, alone in a strange country with a continental car (that I had to drive on the wrong side of the road) to a hotel that had been booked for me, but where I knew not, with my only companion a huge bunch of keys that despite his two-minute explanation left me more confused

13

than before he started. There was only one thing to do and that was to go to the church, confess my weakness and pray for strength to cope with the future.

By now darkness had fallen. I locked up the mission and made my way to the car. Once inside, I tried to acclimatise myself to its workings before setting off to a destination I knew not where and driving, for the first time in my life, on the wrong side of the road. It became a nightmare journey and just when I thought things couldn't get any worse, they did. The hooting of cars, the urgent waving of hands, people shouting at me in a language I didn't understand convinced me that something was wrong. It didn't take me long to realise that I was going the wrong way down a one-way street! It took several attempts before I managed to get the car into reverse and began the long and tortuous reversal out of a seemingly endless one-way street. The relief at finally booking into the hotel was immense, but it wasn't until I had a couple of drinks in the bar that I returned to some measure of normality.

I had called for a staff meeting the following morning, which was attended by everyone except my assistant chaplain. This was probably a good thing as the first job was to blitz the office, clearing chairs that could then be sat on, a desk that had space on it and changing the furniture around to make a more presentable appearance. It took six of us some three hours to clean and transform the room and get rid of the piles of rubbish, which took us up to lunchtime. As a reward, I offered to take them all out for a Chinese meal. I had an awful job in making the waiter understand what I wanted. That he didn't was evident when the order came. Amongst to the various dishes he brought to the table were six large bowls of rice, over three quarters of which remained untouched. As I was footing the bill, no one apart from me seemed to care, but, cost apart, it proved to be a good PR exercise. Enthusiasm waned somewhat after lunch, but as it was mainly a case of finishing touches by 5.00 p.m. the job was completed.

'Well done, everybody,' I told them. 'Time to go home, so have the rest of the day off.'

My licensing as chaplain, the next item on the agenda, was a very moving occasion, taking place in a crowded church, followed by a very warm and friendly reception. The Bishop of Europe presided over the ceremony, which was also attended by many visiting clergy, as

My licensing by the Bishop of Europe, 1983.

St Mary's choir.

15

well as members of my family and friends. I was very much heartened by it all and felt strengthened to tackle all that lay ahead. I was very pleased to see the strength of the choir, whose singing greatly enhanced the service. Wherever I have served where there is a choir, I have always looked upon them as members of the team and their presence alone was a great blessing. One member confided in me that there was a paedophile in the choir, but who was always heavily sedated, so was no threat to anyone.

SETTLING IN

With my work space now transformed and fully functioning, I decided the next task was to visit the other missions in and around Rotterdam, for which I was responsible, familiarise myself with their workings and get a sense of the layout of the vast port. It took me weeks just to find my way around, but as I did I realised that it would be impossible for me to operate in the same way as I had in Dar es Salaam and Bangkok. Just to visit each mission in turn took me the whole day, let alone visits to the ships in the area, which are and always will be the core of the mission's work.

Back in the main mission, I sat down to try and work out some strategy. No sooner had I started than the Church wardens of St Mary's church came to see me and reminded me that my time was to be divided approximately 55% mission and 45% St Mary's. They pointed out that it was the only Anglican Church in Rotterdam so there was huge scope for outreach, which they hoped I would regard as top priority. There was a full programme of services, which they expected to be maintained, indeed, if possible, increased! They also told me that the finances of the church were poor and that some form of stewardship was urgently required! They informed me that as St Mary's paid some of my salary, to put it bluntly, they wanted their pound of flesh! This was news to me and indeed to head office. Didn't they study the annual accounts? I wryly asked them. I also discovered that the Catholic Apostolic Church held a monthly service at St Mary's, for which I would receive an honorarium. Head office were not aware of this either.

After they left I tried to take in all they had told me. I also did some figures regarding my salary and after totting up all the sources, came to see that I earned more money than anyone else in the mission, including the general secretary himself.

An example of their generosity arose when thieves broke into the vestry and took away my sick communion set. No sooner had they heard about my loss than they went out and bought me a new one.

Another thought then struck me. My new assistant colleague had not only been demoted, his income would drop considerably, whereas mine would increase, which was probably another reason why he and his wife were so incensed. I pointed out to head office that without these two increases, my salary was adequate whereas, with young children, my colleague would no doubt be struggling. I therefore suggested that the money from St Mary's be allowed to continue, but be given to him and not me. Head office agreed to this and that's what happened.

ST MARY'S BACKGROUND HISTORY

Before moving on, I feel it would be helpful to provide some background history of St Mary's, an Anglican church in the middle of Rotterdam, and also the three missions which completed the complex. To do so we need to go back to the end of the sixteenth century. By that time there were many British people scattered around the country; including those involved with manufactured cloth and woollen goods. There were also English and Scots troops helping to maintain Holland's newly declared independence from Spain. There were also several clergy, who had fled from their native land on account of their religious beliefs to Holland, the very cradle of the Reformation. The clergy, having no superiors, did very much what they liked, which caused great concern to the hierarchy in England. A series of actions eventually brought the clergy in Holland under the discipline of the Church of England.

You will recall that this was the time of Cromwell in England. The extent of control that the bishops had over the Church in Rotterdam can be seen in the following. It was written by a close friend of the chaplain at that time.

It must have been a very unhappy day for our minister, the Rev. George Beaumont, who has guided his flock since 1635, to be forced to remove 'the Holy communion table', to break down the holy rails. Remove the sanctuary, all in use in accordance with the Holy Rites and Orders of the Bishops of England. All was

17

St Mary's Church, 1832.

taboo, and had to be thrown out. Everything had to become properly independent, in style and worship.

The history of the present Anglican community begins only in 1697 when a group of people agreed to meet the salary of an episcopal clergyman. They met for worship in a converted warehouse before raising funds to build a chapel, which was consecrated in 1708. A lot of the funds were subscribed by the captains of the London and Dublin vessels, thus showing the Church's very close link with the seafaring community. The church flourished for some ninety years, until the French invasion meant the departure of the chaplain and misuse of the chapel. It wasn't until 1878 that a new chaplain was appointed. By this time, Rotterdam, as a port, was rapidly developing and the ever-increasing number of ships using the harbour made it imperative that some provision ashore should be available for the crews. The Missions to Seamen was invited to undertake this vital work, and thus in 1893 the famous flag of the flying angel was hoisted over the building on the Boomers, on the banks of the River Maas. The church, in the meantime, was falling into disrepair and it was decided to build a new church next door to the mission building on the Pieter de Hoochweg. The foundation stone was laid in 1913.

The Missions to Seamen flag was hoisted in 1893 on the Boomers on the banks of the
River Maas. St Mary's church was added in 1913 to the right of the Mission.

World War I saw the church being used to house those who were
interned and it was only afterwards that church and mission were
restored and brought back into normal use. The outbreak of the Second
World War yet again disrupted the church's work, as many expats left
for England. The church and mission was used to house German troops
and later for storing petrol and motorcycles.

With the end of the war, a service of thanksgiving was held on 12th
May 1945, followed by restoration works. With the departure of the
army chaplains, the Rev. W. Popham Hosford was appointed as the
Missions to Seamen chaplain. He will always be remembered as the
most well-known and respected of all the chaplains (including me)
who have served as the incumbent at Rotterdam.

The church congregation increased at this time due to the fact that
Dutch servicemen, merchant seamen and civilians working in England
had married British girls. The expanding port also demanded attention;
in 1948 the mission opened a new club at the Wilton Fijenoord dockyard
at Schiedam, a godsend for the crews whose ships were laid up in dry

St Mary's reredos today.

dock. The great oil installations at Pernis were extending also, and in 1951 another club was opened on the banks of the River Maas and was much used and appreciated by the 'tanker crews'. To complete the picture a fine new launch was added to the facilities that the mission had to offer. This brief history shows how excellent the facilities that the mission had to offer were during the time of Popham Hosford and immediately afterwards. But time and tide wait for no man, which meant that I had an awful amount of catching up to do if I could reproduce the mission's former glory. What follows is the record of six years of effort. The result? Like the curate's egg: good in parts!

One of my first priorities was to tackle the financial situation. I knew that the intention as far as the port committee was concerned was to close the work down and that I only had one year to turn it round. The second task was to rationalise the sites of the three missions: namely, the central building at Pieter de Hoochweg and the clubs at Pernis and Schiedam.

THE MISSION AT PIETER DE HOOCHWEG

The main mission on the side of the River Maas, which was by far the largest of the three, was, due to the relocation of the shipping to new container berths some thirteen miles away, now in the wrong place and needed to be closed. But there were huge complications, particularly because St Mary's Church was situated on the plot adjoining it. By closing the mission, the church, with its vestry and meeting hall on the mission site, would lose them both, an impossible situation. The long-term objective was still to close it down, but that couldn't be done until arrangements safeguarding the church could be made. The question of the dire financial situation intruded into every thought, so any plan had to take in the problem of costing.

Then came my first break. I heard that Rotterdam Council was planning to open up nursery schools so that young mothers could go to work. I contacted the office concerned and suggested that the mission's hall would be perfect for a nursery. They came, they saw and we conquered! With various alterations, which they would pay for, our premises would be perfect. The church and vestry were not part of the nursery, so remained available at all times. The income was substantial and not only covered the church's costs, but left a surplus. So came about the first step in solving the financial crisis that had hung like a huge black cloud over everything connected with the mission.

THE WELFARE OF THE STAFF

The financial crisis aside, it was a priority to consider the welfare of the staff. Not unsurprisingly, morale was low and my number two was obviously very unhappy with the situation he found himself in. Understandably so, but it made my task even more difficult. I made it abundantly clear to head office that the situation couldn't continue indefinitely and this they acknowledged. He was appointed *pro tem* the chaplain for Schiedam. The four student helpers, likewise, were unhappy with their accommodation. I had already promised that I would find them alternate accommodation as soon as possible, but there were many wheels that needed oiling before I could bring that about.

There were other problems. For example, one of our senior chaplains serving in an overseas port wanted to return the UK as his daughter was entering university and he wanted to be near her. Unfortunately there were no vacancies in any of the UK ports, so reluctantly he applied and was accepted for a parish within the Church in Wales. Then, only a couple of days before his induction, it came to light that this was his second marriage, following a divorce from his first wife, so the appointment was cancelled. His first wife had a mental breakdown shortly after they were married and was permanently institutionalised. Separation led to divorce. Sometime later he met and then married his second wife. They had been happily married for over twenty years, were universally respected, with no blemish on the character of either of them. The Church in Wales at that time had a policy of no divorcees holding any position in the Church. They also, incidentally, wouldn't accept any ordained women either. One can hardly imagine their distress when having resigned from the mission and expecting to move into the vicarage within the week, they suddenly found themselves without a job and with no house to move into. On top of this they were completely gutted at the re-emergence of the breakdown of the marriage, all in such distressing circumstances.

Head office shared in their distress and vowed to help them out. The mission at Pernis was at that time without a chaplain so head office offered him the vacancy, which he gratefully accepted. The trouble was that it was totally unsuitable for him at his time of life. Pernis was a large oil refinery, miles from anywhere, and was really suitable only for a young chaplain starting out in his ministry. His previous mission was one of the most important in the society and his status there reflected this fact. The Pernis accommodation on the other hand was suitable for a junior clergyman, so proved a let-down for them both. There were also other problems; the smell of the oil refinery penetrated everywhere and was unpleasant to say the least; oil tankers weren't the easiest of ships to visit and required the energy of a young person, which he certainly wasn't; Holland, although not far from the UK, was too expensive for regular visits, either for themselves or their daughter. I, for my part, was at first delighted to have a chaplain at Pernis, but that pleasure quickly turned into dismay when I learnt of their unhappiness. I went to see them and it was immediately obvious that they were desperately unhappy. They couldn't sleep at night and the odour of the oil refinery made them both ill. I was so concerned for their wellbeing that I flew to head office, who agreed that they must be moved. So it was that a few weeks later I wished them good bye and good luck as they returned to England and, through the good offices of mission contacts, to a living in the Lincoln Diocese.

To divert for a moment, the Port of Rotterdam complex had the largest staff of any port in the world. This had its pros and cons. It inevitably meant a regular movement of personnel. This sometimes led to unsuitable appointments by head office, just to fill a slot. The divorced chaplain was a good example. I must have been very unlucky because the following two appointments both proved unsuitable.

THE MISSION AT PERNIS

Because of the continuous changeover of personnel at Pernis, we employed a permanent manager to run the club. This had its disadvantages. In any mission the chaplain was always in charge, but by the very nature of the manager being permanent, and sometimes working without a chaplain, he had his finger on the pulse. He handled all the money, did the ordering for the canteen and organised the necessary maintenance of the building and transport. This of course freed the chaplain so he could concentrate on the spiritual ministry of the mission.

In all the clubs the maintenance of the transport was a huge headache. Every station had a minibus used mainly for picking up seamen from their ships and returning them at the end of their visit. There was a constant changeover of drivers, never a good thing for any vehicle, especially as the students, who drove them more than anyone else, were young and inexperienced. This inevitably resulted in frequent scrapes or accidents, which proved extremely expensive to repair. A South African priest, who replaced the unfortunate divorced padre, suggested to head office that he should buy a large Range Rover, only driven by him, which of course could also pick up seafarers. The trouble was the expense of purchasing such a vehicle, so he was given a budget figure within which he had to operate. He achieved this by going down to Belgium, buying the vehicle there and because he was taking it out of the country, avoiding paying that country's duty. Whether or not he was ignorant of the law, or hoped that no one would realise that he had bought it outside Holland, I do not know, but the fact was that if he kept the vehicle for over six months in the Netherlands then he had to pay Dutch duty. Six months passed and he was actually away in South Africa on leave when the law caught up with him. The vehicle was being driven by one of the students when he was stopped by the police and arrested for driving a vehicle without a Dutch tax certificate. The first I knew about it was when the student rang me from the police station, in great distress and completely unaware that he had been breaking the law. I had great difficulty in convincing the police that the student was in no way to blame and it was only after I accepted responsibility for the vehicle and agreed to pay the fine that they released him. A somewhat chastened priest returned from leave to face the music. He had to pay the fine, but didn't have the money to pay the outstanding duty, so had to take the vehicle back to Belgium. The garage that he bought it from in Belgium would only take it back at a much lower price than he originally paid for it so there was a loss all round. Shortly after the loss of his vehicle, we lost him too as he was transferred to another port. His successor didn't fare much better and also had a short spell of duty before departing, actually getting the sack. He was a very young priest, his most precious belonging being a grand piano, which he insisted on having with him in Pernis. I said the finances of the station, being what they were, couldn't stretch to pay for the cost of bringing it and then returning it at the end of his contract. Head office, who made the appointment, agreed, however, to meet the cost and so it came. He had little conception of the financial straits of working in a mission and demanded that his accommodation be renovated from top to bottom. I pointed out that we had no money to employ a firm, but would meet the cost of materials for him to do the work, to which he agreed. Because of other pressures I had more or less to leave him to it and as I heard nothing, presumed that no news was good news. Alas, it was not!

The club manager reported that he was no longer able to balance the books as money seemed to be missing from the till. He had noticed that the priest was going to the till and questioned him about the shortage. The reply he received was that the banks in the UK hadn't fixed up the exchange of his salary yet, so he was short of cash. The manager asked him to put a chitty in for any money taken, but despite this there was still money short. When questioned again he said that he took money for decorating, etc., so didn't feel it necessary to record this. Actually he came shortly before I was leaving and held the fort before a new senior chaplain was appointed. I am not sure what happened but he was sacked shortly afterwards and moved on.

SCHIEDAM MISSION

Possibly the biggest problem of all arose from the mission in Schiedam, situated in the grounds of Schiedam Dockyard. At a time when things were good at the dockyard, the owners built a seaman's club and asked the Missions to Seamen to run it. They agreed to maintain the building, which meant that the only cost was the payment of staff. The mission was very popular, especially for the crews of the ships in dry dock, because many of the facilities of the ships were closed down during dry docking. Soon after I arrived, I noticed that parts of the building were in a very dilapidated state and needed urgent attention. I made myself known to the yard owners and thanked them for their generous help. I then mentioned that a lot of work needed to be undertaken to bring the club up to scratch. I was shattered when they told me that the dockyard had fallen on hard times, that money was very short and sadly they had no cash available to make repairs. They added that they would no longer be able to maintain the building, and if it were to remain open then that responsibility would fall upon the society. This news was immediately passed to the mission treasurer, who called a special meeting of the port committee with the recommendation that the club be closed.

I had recently met the general secretary of the Dutch Seamen's Union and got on well with him. He was most appreciative of the mission's work and said if I ever needed any help to let him know. In desperation, I went to him and told him of the developments at Schiedam, which meant almost certainly the club's closure. I had obtained a rough estimate of the amount needed to restore the club, so when he asked me how much was needed I was able to tell him. He made no promises, but that he would raise the matter with his executive officers and if he had any good news he would let me know. The day of the emergency port committee dawned, with no message from the union, so it was with a very heavy heart that I prepared to meet them shortly. Just as I was preparing to leave, the phone rang. Unbelievably it was the general secretary of the Seamen's Union. I could hardly believe my ears when he told me that the union had agreed to pay for the cost of restoration, plus a little extra to meet any contingencies. I hadn't mentioned to any of the port committee my efforts to raise funds, nor had I time to tell them of the change in fortune! The chairman opened the meeting by saying this would be one of the shortest meetings on record. There was only one item on the agenda and only one possible answer, to close the club down. I don't think I have ever enjoyed five minutes more at a meeting than those that followed. In as matter-of-fact a way as possible, I told them the good news. It was greeted with stunned silence. I had another ace up my sleeve. I had earlier called a meeting of all the churches in Schiedam, seeking a rota of volunteers to replace the paid member of staff, running the canteen and shop, and, praise to the Lord, I got it! The union paid for the restoration, the volunteers took on the running of the canteen and shop, and Schiedam became one of the friendliest clubs ever. The system of volunteers exists to this day and as a result, the club became and remains financially viable. Long after I left Rotterdam, the dockyard, now on a firm footing, built a new club. I was a privileged guest when Princess Anne, who is the patron of the Mission to Seafarers (as it is now called), opened the new building.

It is well worth recording here the wonderful support the Princess Royal, our president, has given and still gives to the work of the Missions to Seafarers. I met her no less than four times whilst in Holland: in the main mission at Rotterdam, at our stations at Vlissingen and Schiedam, and after the Zeebrugge Disaster.

Princess Anne visiting the Vlissingen Mission.

THE SINKING OF THE *HERALD OF FREE ENTERPRISE* AT ZEEBRUGGE

The mission staff became very involved over the sinking of the *Herald of Free Enterprise*. I received a telephone call from a contact at the Zeebrugge port very shortly after the disaster occurred. I immediately informed all the clergy in the area and then set off with my assistant chaplain for about a three-hour drive to the port. When we arrived at the gates, police were controlling the entrance and many vehicles were being turned away. But such is the power of the dog collar, we were immediately waved through and directed to where an emergency meeting was being held. The clergy present were divided into three: one group was sent to where the rescuers were being landed and the second to the makeshift mortuary. The third group, including me, covered the hospitals where the wounded had been taken. There was a constant stream of activity in the mortuary as more and more bodies were being brought in. I decided that I would go to the main hospital where the injured, including the captain and some members of the crew, had been taken.

I was immediately directed to the captain's room, but had to wait to see him as he was being interviewed by the police. As soon as they left, I was taken in. I spoke earlier about the power of the dog collar. Mine was the first thing he noticed and its presence was remarkable. The captain had suffered some broken ribs and was obviously in considerable pain. Nevertheless my presence brought a smile to his face and as I approached his bed, he said, 'A friendly face. How wonderful to see you, Padre.' He wanted to know the state of his ship but I skirted around that one, saying I had come direct to him, so wasn't sure. We shared in prayer and then I asked him if there was anything I could do for him? There was. Could I ring his wife in the UK and tell her he was not badly injured. I left him to phone and luckily got through straightaway. His wife had only just learnt of the accident by a news flash on the television, so I was able to update her about the state of her husband and where he was in hospital. She obviously wanted to come to Holland and I agreed to meet her at the airport and take her to the hotel, which I reserved for her. From there, I could take her to her husband in hospital. All these arrangements took considerable time to implement, but were made easier by the hospital putting phones at my disposal.

This meant that I was still at the hospital some three hours later, when I discovered almost for certain what had caused the tragedy. It was the bosun's job to make sure that the bow doors of the ship were locked down before the ferry moved off. Time was always of the essence on the ferries, which meant that the timing had to be perfect. The bosun had been drinking so delegated the task to one of his subordinates. He unfortunately fell asleep so the doors were not closed. Water rushed in and within a very short time the ship heeled over with disastrous consequences. The man responsible was also injured and was in the same hospital as the captain. At some time during his stay there, he came to realise that the tragedy had occurred because he had not done his job. The quietness of the hospital was shattered as he went screaming down one corridor after another shouting he was to blame. He was eventually sedated, but by now it was obvious to everyone who heard him, including me, that he was indeed to blame. A precaution since, incidentally, has been to have cameras installed on the bridge, covering the bow doors, ensuring that a similar situation could not recur.

The television crews were in abundance and spoke to one young lady whose fiancé was missing. She was very brave on camera but once the crews had moved on she broke down and wept. I did what I could to comfort her, while we waited for more information. One of the tasks that had fallen to the chaplains was to go to the morgue with details of those missing, to see if they could be identified. Sadly her fiancé was one such person.

Princess Anne, either by choice or chance, was shortly afterwards in the area and asked to see those clergy who had helped during the crisis. So it came to pass that some six of us had over half an hour with the princess in a private room. There was a posed photo of Anne and me, which unfortunately was one that got away! I am on permanent record, however, as the salvage company produced a thirty-minute film of the tragedy, including a service at sea. My contribution was recorded on their official cover.

Princess Anne was not the only royal visitor that I met in Rotterdam. Prince Andrew and Sarah Ferguson attended St Mary's Church shortly after they were married. All did not go well, however. In the UK, if on an official visit with royalty, traffic lights are ignored, but not so in Holland. As a result, at a red light, the royal car crashed into the car ahead of it! A less than dignified couple alighted from the car at the church, only to be taken in hand by the British Ambassador, Sir John Margetson (who readers of my book will recognise as a friend

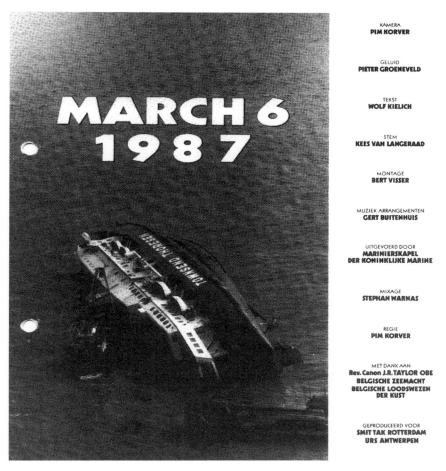

KAMERA
PIM KORVER

GELUID
PIETER GROENEVELD

TEKST
WOLF KIELICH

STEM
KEES VAN LANGERAAD

MONTAGE
BERT VISSER

MUZIEK ARRANGEMENTEN
GERT BUITENHUIS

UITGEVOERD DOOR
**MARINIERSKAPEL
DER KONINKLIJKE MARINE**

MIXAGE
STEPHAN WARNAS

REGIE
PIM KORVER

MET DANK AAN
**Rev. Canon J.R. TAYLOR OBE
BELGISCHE ZEEMACHT
BELGISCHE LOODSWEZEN
DER KUST**

GEPRODUCEERD VOOR
**SMIT TAK ROTTERDAM
URS ANTWERPEN**

The sinking of the *Herald of Free Enterprise*, Zeebrugge.

of mine going back to the Vietnam and Thailand days). Furthermore, it was obvious that Andrew and Sarah were unhappy, having recently had a tiff. I tried to lighten the atmosphere by saying to Sarah, 'You should support the mission whenever possible.'

'Why?' she replied.

I told her, 'Because we chaplains try to keep all sailors on the straight and narrow, and that includes Prince Andrew!'

After the service was over, I escorted them to the back of the church. There were many children in the congregation and they all had posies to give to Sarah as she passed by. Sarah turned to Andrew and said, 'What am I supposed to do with all these?'

29

'Give them to your lady in waiting, of course,' he replied. 'Why on earth else do you think she is here?'

After the service there were the usual photographs, with me rather splendid in the cape the Archbishop John gave to me in Tanzania. Photos were reprinted in many papers and ladies' magazines; in most of them I was mistaken for the bishop! I subsequently had a memorandum from head office addressed to 'An Imposter'. By the side of the photo were the words, 'Star of stage, screen and women's weekly!' And below, 'It is a criminal offence to impersonate a bishop!!'

As things seem to come in threes, I must tell you about a third meeting with royalty: namely, Princess Margaret. I was invited to an official function followed by lunch at the Embassy. For some reason the ambassador had to stay on after the ceremony so he asked me if

Prince Andrew and Sarah, Duchess of York at St Mary's.

I could go back directly to the Embassy and to entertain Princess Margaret until he arrived. He thought we would be on our own for about ten minutes. If the truth be known, whilst I was growing up, I had a crush on Margaret (we were the same age) and I was musing on this when in she walked, smoking a cigarette, with a flunkey carrying

The Duchess of York after the service.

an ashtray. Conversation was hard-going, interrupted as she frequently turned around to deposit ash in the ashtray provided for her. So it was with no small sense of relief when the ambassador entered shortly afterward and took over.

At lunch the Archbishop of Canterbury was also present, but he was much easier to talk to. One of the great privileges of being a priest is that no matter whom you meet, be they VIPs or ordinary people, in your eyes they are all equally important. I am thinking particularly at this moment of an alcoholic seaman that used the mission at Pieter de Hochberg every day. His days at sea were finished but he still loved the mission. The Dutch Authorities seemed to have a more sympathetic approach to alcoholics than we do. As far as I understood, the Authority gave him the money to buy a couple of beers a day and then laid on a taxi to take him safely home. His liver eventually gave up the fight and I was asked to take his funeral. I then discovered that he had no relatives, no money and no next of kin. This meant a pauper's funeral.

I was agreeably surprised to find, however, that apart from finding a suitable time for the undertaker's, he was afforded a traditional service. The only setback was that it was scheduled for first thing in the morning, which I thought wouldn't suit most mourners. Additionally, as he had no relatives or next of kin, I thought it quite possible that, apart from the undertakers and myself, there would be no one else there. I was wrong. Just before the hearse arrived, five of his drinking friends turned up. The contrast between their clothes and the undertaker's brought a smile to my lips. The undertaker and pall bearers were all in morning dress, whereas his friends appeared in clothes that hadn't seen the cleaner's benefits for longer than one cared to think! We arrived at the cemetery and the solemn procession to the graveside began. The pall bearers were immaculate and in perfect step. His friends (not one seemed to be walking in a straight line) staggered along as best they could. Their conversation was unlike any I have ever heard at a funeral. I told them to be quiet as I led the service at the graveside and most of them were, except that there were loud 'Amens' when there should have been silence and silence where there should have been an 'Amen!' At the end of the service the undertaker stood with a container of earth in case anyone wanted to sprinkle some on the

Suffer the little children to come unto me.

coffin, but his friends had other ideas. Some had long conversations with him and without exception, instead of earth, they dropped bottles of beer, his favourite tunes on CDs and a couple of magazines. Throughout all this, the bearers stood without showing any signs of anything being amiss, although, like me, I suspect they breathed a sigh of relief when it was all over.

I have already mentioned that it was my considered opinion that being senior chaplain of the Missions to Seamen in the largest port in the world, being secretary for the Netherlands and chaplain of St Mary's, the only Anglican Church in Rotterdam, was just too much for one priest. I had not been in the post for very long before this became very evident. True, as far as the mission was concerned, there were additional staff, but it needed a senior chaplain to coordinate activities, to oversee the whole operation as well as play an active part in the work itself. St Mary's was the only Anglican Church in Rotterdam, the largest city in the Netherlands. It had a regular congregation of between fifty and sixty souls, but the opportunity for expansion was obvious. I have also mentioned that the main mission with the church adjoining it was now in the wrong position, due to its distance from where the ships now berthed. But to close the mission would affect the church, as its vestry and meeting area was in the mission itself. There was another huge problem. The mission provided the house for the chaplain and paid his salary. If St Mary's was to have its own priest then he would need a house and his salary would, in part at least, have to be met by the congregation. With its potential for expansion I felt sure that the money could be forthcoming, although the question remained of the church being handicapped by losing its vestry and hall if the mission closed.

Then, out of the blue (or should I say in answer to prayer), came a possible solution. An 'Old Catholic Church' was sited about a mile from the mission, but in a much more pleasant area. St Mary's Church, alongside the mission, was now housed in what had become a rundown area. The building was often broken into by thieves and on one Sunday the church bells were ringing as usual for the 11.00 a.m. service when a neighbour who disliked the noise threw a brick through the church window!

The Old Catholic Church was badly damaged during the war but was beautifully restored after. Furthermore, it boasted its own house for its priest, as well as a church hall for meetings. With age its congregation dwindled so a decision was made by the elders that the

33

church should be closed down. I had become very friendly with the elders and shared my problems with them. They were determined that their church should not be used for anything other than worship, otherwise to be razed to the ground. I was thrilled beyond measure when a meeting of the elders decided that they would give the church and house to us for absolutely nothing, as long as it continued to be used as a church.

I had kept my church wardens in the picture, who amazingly didn't seem too enthusiastic, possibly because they didn't think we would be offered it for nothing. But it was and we were formally offered the church complete with house and hall, all for nothing, the only condition being that the complex continued as a church. They also agreed that if we didn't accept then the church and house would be razed to the ground.

St Mary's was a brick church, as indeed was the Old Catholic. The only difference was that, because it was considerably larger than St Mary's, there was more brickwork! I couldn't believe what I was hearing when members of my congregation started complaining that they didn't like it because it was a brick church! That complaint signalled an avalanche of others. I knew the writing was on the wall when one of the leading families in the congregation, whose parents had put the pews in St Mary's, demanded that they had to be moved over to the new church. But the knockout blow came when the organist insisted that the organ from St Mary's be moved to the new church! This, despite the fact that their organ was superior to St Mary's.

Everyone was aware that I believed St Mary's should have its own full-time priest. Some agreed but the problem of there being no house for the priest was the main stumbling block. Then came this wonderful offer, but to my amazement it was turned down. Their church was indeed razed to the ground very shortly afterwards and the plot of land sold.

COMBINING CHURCH AND MISSION

To date I have concentrated on my work at St Mary's. But, in fact, my appointment to Rotterdam was by the Missions to Seafarers. In this second volume I have said nothing about the main core of the mission's work. That always took priority, which I executed as closely as I could. Its work can be summed up as being that part of the Anglican Communion which 'cares for the spiritual, material and mental

34

welfare of all seafarers, irrespective of nationality, colour or creed'. No matter where the station is situated, be it in the UK or abroad, the core of the work is the same. In *A Man with a Mission* many such examples are described in detail.

It is not surprising, therefore, that my favourite mission prayer is the following:

Bless the Missions to Seafarers and all who work for them.
Keep their welcome warm and their love and care unstinting,
May their ministry to seafarers express the love of Christ for all.
Amen.

This prayer encompasses the length, breadth and depth of God's love for all his people, whether in the mission's chapel or on board ships, in hospital, prison or homes, by taking services or any other form of ministry, where needed. For the record, I have partaken in most. These include counselling, hearing confessions or just listening; taking services on a regular basis in the mission chapel and on occasions on board ships; providing phone booths so that Seafarers can ring loved ones at home in private; writing letters on behalf of or for seafarers (still today some are illiterate); taking up a seafarer's cause with ship owners, unions or clergy in other ports or at the seafarer's home; running a mission, including ordering the necessities to provide for the comforts and needs of people using it; transporting seafarers from ship to shore; taking them to places of interest or need; providing libraries and exchanging books when needed; arranging sports fixtures and transporting teams to the necessary destinations; making up numbers when needed and refereeing matches; providing sports equipment (including the gear, i.e. footballs or golf clubs); shopping for a seafarer who can't get ashore for himself; preparing seafarers for baptism and baptising them; the same with confirmation classes, often with lessons held in different ports (this is achieved by all chaplains having the same outline of instructions, with the candidate being passed onto the chaplain at the next port of call); and last but by no means least, visiting seamen in hospitals and prisons.

As already explained, apart from my work as port chaplain, I was also chaplain to St Mary's Church. My time was in theory to be roughly evenly divided between the two. Both tasks really demanded a full-time ministry, but in practice, whatever situation arose, I gave it my undivided attention until the day I left. Some situations were ongoing and continued even after I left Rotterdam. Two of them (at least) are worth recording.

RON

The first is centred on Ron. Why I'm not recording his surname will become obvious as the story unfolds. I was working in my office one morning when a knock on the door interrupted progress on a report I was preparing. My visitor was unknown to me, although I was struck by his size – well over 6-foot tall and a body to match it. I invited him to sit down wondering what he might need help with, but never in a hundred years was I expecting the words that came from his lips.

'Do you do confirmations?' he asked me.

Not only was I surprised by his question, but also in the way he asked me. Rather like one might ask a butcher, 'Do you sell meat?'

'Yes,' was all I could muster in response. He then proceeded to enlighten me as to why he was sitting in my office. He had a daughter who was very keen on riding. Her dearest possession was her horse, which she rode almost every day, specialising in jumping. She was practising in a field near her home when she attempted to jump the gate, but things went horribly wrong. The jump failed and in the process her horse was badly gashed on one side. Treatment by the vet failed to cure the horse; indeed, it became worse as an infection took over. So much so that the vet said the only thing to do was to put the horse down. His daughter was distraught and Ron begged the vet to delay for two more days. Ron was not a practising Christian but in desperation he prayed to God to heal the horse. He made a vow that if the horse was healed he would become a practising Christian! To his, the vet's and his daughter's relief, an immediate healing occurred. To honour his vow to God, he was now asking me for confirmation.

I explained that before he could be confirmed he had to attend classes and church, but the more I put forward rules and regulations the more determined he became, and in the end I agreed to prepare him for confirmation. He attended every class, he attended church regularly and also offered to help in any way he could.

As already explained, the finances of the church and mission were in a dire state and one way to raise funds was by raffles. As in most church raffles, the prizes were pretty ordinary, until Ron came on the scene. He explained that he made a living by buying up odd lots of unwanted stock and then selling them off at a profit. As a result he had many items of value and interest, which made perfect prizes for our raffles. He entered fully into the life of the church and actually came onto the PCC. He brought a freshness of ideas to the meetings (not all, of course, were acceptable) and everyone liked him. If the truth be known, he was really a failed entrepreneur and I suspected sometimes had had to sail close to the wind to survive. As a consequence, his fortunes fluctuated, sometimes he seemed affluent, but on other occasions literally broke. He had a family in the UK but rented a small house on the outskirts of Rotterdam. On more than one occasion I used to take food for him and his cat at his house. His wife used to come to Holland from time to time and one sensed there wasn't a great deal of love between them, although I was never asked for counselling or advice. Ron always seemed on the move, travelling between Holland and the UK, as well as the neighbouring countries, including Germany, Belgium and France. On one occasion he returned from Germany and presented me with a very expensive-looking cutlery set. It was housed in a beautiful leather case, which I use still today. It was a present he told me for preparing and having him confirmed.

He was a supreme optimist, always coming up with the promise of some huge deal in the pipeline, which sadly never seemed to materialise. In many ways he was just like Del Boy – 'This time next year I'll be a millionaire!' I grew very fond of him and felt quite sad when the time came for us to leave Holland and return to the UK. He promised, however, to keep in touch when in the UK and was as good as his word, often just turning up and telling of a huge deal that he was in the process of completing, which never seeming to materialise.

BILL, HIS WIFE AND SOME MORE OF RON

Leaving aside for a moment the saga of Ron, I want to tell you about Bill and his wife. Bill was a Dutchman who worshipped at St Mary's and was more British in his ways and mannerisms than many Englishmen. He wanted to be ordained but because of his age and other reasons, I knew that his wish would not be fulfilled. But he did help in many ways, including visiting criminals in prison. His wife didn't attend worship because she was confined to a wheelchair and was in fact terminally ill. At her request I used to take sick communion to her on a regular basis. Even after we left Rotterdam she used to beg me to continue and I did in fact travel over to administer sick communion. On one occasion, Ron turned up unexpectedly at Warnham and after greetings and an update on his fortunes, it transpired that he was returning shortly to Rotterdam. Hearing I was also going he offered to take me in his car and put me up at the same hotel at which he was going to stay. No charge, he told me, as all expenses for the trip would be met from his business account. Sure enough, about a week later, he picked me up and off we went to Rotterdam. The journey was uneventful and once installed in the hotel, we went about our separate ways. We stayed for about three days and then set off on the return journey. We went home by a different route and port because, as Ron explained, the customs at Dover always gave him a rough time. They were suspicious, he told me, because he made so many journeys to Rotterdam and back. The customs in fact waved us through without any bother and he duly dropped me back home and went on his way.

About a month later, I received a frantic phone call from Ron's wife who told me that Ron had been arrested and charged with smuggling drugs into the country. I later received a phone call from his barrister asking me if I would give him a character reference at his trial, to which I agreed. I duly attended the court and spoke on his behalf, but not before his barrister rang me again and said he was with Ron in his car on the way to the court. He asked me if I knew that Ron had been in prison before, to which I replied no. He then said he had told Ron that he must tell me himself about his previous convictions. Ron came on the phone and to my amazement, told me that he had been in prison twice before, once on a fraud case and another time for some other crime, the details of which I have now forgotten.

So came the time when I appeared in court to give my character reference. Before I could start the judge asked me if I knew of his previous convictions, to which I replied that I had only just now received the news. The judge then asked me had I ever travelled to Rotterdam and back with Ron, to which I replied in the affirmative.

'Yes, we know,' said the judge. Ron had been under surveillance for some time and we were followed by police for the whole of the journey that we took together. At one time the police wondered if I was an accomplice in the drug smuggling crime, but when they learnt of the reason I had gone to Rotterdam, I was cleared of all suspicion. According to the prosecution, Ron had sent a lorry load of vegetables containing drugs into the country. The police followed the lorry to a warehouse in Liverpool that Ron used. He was waiting there when the lorry arrived and started unloading the contents when the police swooped, catching Ron red-handed. There was no doubt of his guilt and he was duly sentenced to a long spell in prison. I visited him regularly in his gaol in Liverpool and couldn't help but notice the difference (for the good) between prisons in Africa and Thailand, as recorded in *A Man with a Mission*. After serving about a year of his sentence, Ron was found to be riddled with cancer and was released on compassionate grounds. He died shortly afterwards, so ending a sad and sorry episode in the life of Ron. A failed but loving character.

In the meantime, I still travelled to Rotterdam at the request of Bill's wife, taking her communion. The last time I saw her it became obvious to me that her health was failing fast and that she wasn't going to be with us much longer. I asked Bill to keep me in touch, which he did, but partly because of his Dutch and also because of my poor hearing, I sometimes found it difficult to understand all he said. One day, about a fortnight after my last visit, Bill rang me. I thought he said that his wife died last Thursday and even as I offered up my condolences, I thought it strange (in view of the fact that he contacted me so regularly) that he hadn't told me earlier. As the conversation continued I suddenly realised that he was not saying that she died last Thursday, but rather that she was *going* to die next Thursday. He explained that after an early supper together she would go to bed. Then at 8.30 p.m. the doctor would come and give her a fatal injection. She would then die shortly afterwards (euthanasia being allowed in the Netherlands). Bill told me that shortly before the doctor turned up she would ring me, which she did. She sounded very calm and collected, which was more than I could say about myself, wished me good bye and rang off. Still to this day I am not sure of my views on euthanasia. I know it is illegal in this country, but it is a topic to be debated nevertheless.

REFUGEES

As I have given so many examples of a padre's work in his ministry in *A Man with a Mission*, I have deliberately refrained from repeating such instances now, although the reader can rest assured that they were there in Rotterdam also. Two instances not experienced in Hong Kong, Tanzania, or Thailand, however, are worth recording now. Both instances concern refugees. It came with a sense of relief upon leaving Thailand that I would no longer be heavily involved in trying to help refugees find a new life. Although I didn't know it at the time, it was publicly acknowledged by refugees fleeing from Burma, Cambodia or Vietnam that providing you can get to Canon John at Christ Church in Bangkok, you will be safe.

Helping such people was always difficult. Probably the hardest to help were the Burmese. Although Burma was in terrible turmoil, it was not regarded as a refugee territory, because the country was not in a state of civil war. Most of them wanted to get to Europe. In helping refugees, whilst not breaking the law, one nevertheless often had to sail close to the wind. To give but one example, a young Burmese male came seeking help who was obviously a well-educated and intelligent person. It transpired that he had recently finished university with a degree in pharmacy. He desperately wanted to get to the UK as he had relations already in the country. The only chance he had of achieving this aim was if he had a job to go to. My mind immediately turned to my elder brother Peter who was a pharmacist, managing three shops in the Potteries. To digress for a moment, because of their plight, such people have no documents, so all one has to go on is what they tell you. Furthermore, one has no means of testing their moral or ethical behaviour, so helping them in their quest for a new life can be fraught with danger. And to involve another person in their plight can unwittingly cause them problems too. Nevertheless, after due thought and prayer, I decided I would ask my brother Peter if he could take him on in his business. He agreed, so armed with this letter, barriers were crossed, moneys raised for his expenditure, a passage arranged and he was on his way. Things did not work out entirely as planned; for a start he turned up with a wife! It soon became obvious to my brother that all he wanted was to be in the UK. Indeed, shortly afterward, he just disappeared from view, no doubt to be absorbed into the Burmese undercover families that were established (if in an illegal way) in the UK. Looking back at this incident, I still wonder if I did the right thing. I console myself that I honoured my side of the bargain and cannot be blamed if he failed in his.

As I have just said, when I left Thailand, it was with a great sense of relief that my work with refugees was over. But it was not to be. On three occasions when I was in Rotterdam, and twice when I was in Warnham, refugees whom I had helped in the past turned up on my doorstep. Most were full of gratitude, but some were still seeking more help from me! The immigration laws in the UK and the Netherlands were far stricter than in Thailand, so apart from helping them a little financially, I could offer little more.

PAUL TUTU

One case I did get involved with, however, involved a stowaway called Paul Tutu who fled from an African country, seeking political asylum, but virtually became a prisoner on board the ship he stowed away on. The ship arrived at the next port of call, which was in Italy, but the authorities refused to let him land as his passport was not stamped with an exit visa. The same thing happened at the next few ports and as a result, both the ship's captain and Paul were becoming extremely desperate. The captain cabled me asking for help. I suggested that he contact the United Nations High Commissioner for Refugees, but for some reason he didn't. I found out that the next port of call was to be in Belgium and ascertained that he was not necessarily *persona non grata* in that country. We were hopeful that the Belgium authorities would let him ashore so that he could renew his application for political asylum. The Belgian authorities, however, proved intractable, despite more cables, phone calls from other ports and the ship at sea. The final call sent by Paul as his ship anchored off Rotterdam was desperate. He asked me if he could jump ship and come to my house. This suggestion I firmly rejected, but assured him that events were moving in the right direction. Success finally came when the Dutch authorities agreed to let him ashore, provided I accepted full responsibility for him, and guaranteed to get him to the United Nations in Belgium. After two delays, the ship finally entered the port of Rotterdam and one of my assistants, Charles Hope, went on board to collect him. There were anxious moments as the authorities minutely examined his documents before finally releasing him into the safe hands of Charles.

It was a jubilant Paul who came to my house where there was a working party assembling and putting together *The Anglican Sphere*, the parish magazine. He came in smiling from ear to ear, which grew even larger as I told him he looked like a piano keyboard! A bottle of wine was hastily opened and then, all sitting around the dining room table, we held a simple service of thanksgiving. When the service was over, Charles drove him to the United Nations offices in Belgium. His last words as he departed were 'Thank you, Thank You, Thank you!' Shortly afterwards I received the following letter from him. His

English and spelling was not all that good, but the sincerity of his letter more than atoned for that:

Thank You, thank you, thank you. This is Paul. I hope that by the grace of God you are strong in health. I am as well very sound and healthy with your help. In fact thinking of having such a loving and helpful father friend like Rev. Taylor makes me feel strong and safe in the name of God.

It all seemed mystic to me when my problem started but I had faith that I would be saved so when I met you I knew at least I had a prolong life. As a matter of fact words wouldn't be enough to thank you, Charles and your assistances but I hope in the name of God you would accept my prayers for you. It's been the greatest help ever in my life and in fact it will stick in my mind for the rest of my life and I promise to keep in touch with you wherever I go. Thank you very much Rev. Taylor, may God our heavenly father keep you safe and strong to help the helpless. Charles brought me safely to Antwerp and everything is moving wonderfully. I went to the United Nations office the following day and it all went as simple as you told me. I was heartily received without a single question...

I include this letter for two reasons: to show how the work of the Mission to seafarers is far-reaching and as evidence of the power of faith and prayer from a Christian in difficult circumstances.

THE CHALLENGES OF A MINISTRY IN ROTTERDAM

'Being a Christian in difficult circumstances' sums up, in many ways, my time in Rotterdam. The challenges just kept coming and often, solving one difficulty opened up another. This meant that I had little or no time to reflect on where I was and how things were going. One of the great things about holidays or breaks is that when you return, as it were with fresh eyes, weaknesses or urgent needs stand out that previously seemed satisfactory. This meant that one was immediately immersed in action, with no time to consider what lay ahead. This being so, the wisdom of creating a five-year plan of action at the start of one's ministry and referring to it meant that one could see where one stood and what needed attention next. My six years in Rotterdam literally flew by with little time to reflect on progress made and before I realised it, the tenure of office was drawing to a close. I was pleasantly surprised, therefore, to receive a letter from the general secretary of the Mission to Seamen, Canon Bill Down, who shortly afterwards became Bishop of Bermuda, who visited us on an official tour shortly before my departure to pastures new. This is what (in part) he wrote:

My Dear John,
First of all I want to say a big thank you for your kind hospitality, and for making me so welcome. I thought that I would write to you by hand, because I want you to know how much I and all of us here appreciate what you have done and are doing in Rotterdam. You have done a wonderful job for the Missions to Seamen, the accommodation for the chaplains, reader and students is excellent, the financial difficulties have been faced and are being solved, and the inter-staff relationships are good.

On the St Mary's front you have coped manfully. For a long time you did not have the benefit of an ordained colleague and you handled the job wonderfully.

For you, John, coping with the toughest job of your ministry at a time when you had personal problems was bound to be tough. But you have tackled everything with your customary vigour, and you have laid solid foundations for the continuing work of St Mary's and the Missions to Seamen. I have nothing but admiration for what you have achieved. You have the great gifts of enthusiasm, ability, charisma and intelligence; you are not afraid of hard work and have the vision to see what needs to be done. Go for it, and the blessing of the Lord is on all you do...

And then there's your next job, which I have in part laid out to you. We want you to stay with us...

I was naturally gratified by his letter, but on the other hand it confirmed what I feared. That the main tenor of my work had been in management and organisation, whereas what I yearned for was a more spiritual ministry. This is not to say that amongst all the management duties there was not spiritual activity, because there was. But because I have already recorded many similar examples of them in *A Man with a Mission*, I will not repeat them here. But what I will add is one or two of my articles taken from the parish magazine *The Anglian Sphere*, under the headings 'The Vicar Writes', which gives some insight into my ministry at St Mary's and the Missions to Seamen during my time in Rotterdam. I need to stress, however, that it wasn't all work and no play, because that makes Jack a dull boy! With that in mind, I wrote in June 1984 about golf!

GOLF

I have just spent a marvellous week's holiday in the Algarve, which any golfers among you will know is wonderful golf country. I played five rounds of golf, including, for the first time in my life, a round on Sunday. If the truth be known I didn't play very well on that day! I wonder how much I was distracted by two nagging thoughts that would not go away. The first: was it true, as so many of my golfing friends have told me, that you don't have to go to church on a Sunday to worship Almighty God? He can also be worshipped on a golf course; the second: was I wrong to have gone to the golf course rather than to church last Sunday?

I came to the following conclusions. Whereas you can worship God on the golf course, one also needs to worship him with fellow Christians in liturgical and sacramental services. To deny this is a 'cop out'. Also I was not wrong in playing golf on a Sunday. Why? Because it has a lot to teach about the Christian way of Life.

For a start, it makes one aware of the beauty of God's creation. One is forced to study contours, trees, bushes and undergrowth (especially!); to be aware of lakes, sand dunes, the wind and the rain; to face the challenge of finishing the eighteen holes, especially if the wheels of the trolley have gone!

The biblical saying 'having put one's hand to the plough and not turning back' certainly applies to the ancient and noble game of golf. Golf has a great deal to teach about etiquette and consideration for one's neighbour.

The Christian life can be compared to an eighteen-hole golf course. Some shots go well, others badly; grace, whether in victory or defeat, is a necessary Christian characteristic. A sustained Christian life requires self-discipline and self-control. So does golf. 'Well done thou good and faithful servant; enter thou into the joy of the Lord' is how the good book puts it. Relaxing after the game with a refreshing drink in good company is the golfer's equivalent.

But above all, golf is the fairest of all games because of its handicap system. A handicap makes allowances and can even result in victory, rather like God's grace and forgiveness, being a reward for effort. In conclusion perhaps I must also admit that there is some justification for the claims of Sunday golf!

BAPTISM

In June 1988, I wrote:

The story unfolds something like this: The telephone rang (inevitably during my lunch hour) and an unknown voice said, 'Can I have my baby done? Or do you do baptisms at your place?'

Knowing from past experience, this meant that a non-church-going family, for one reason or another, wanted their baby done! Such baptisms are becoming very popular, particularly for so-called partners with no wedding ceremony; the birth of a baby becomes the perfect occasion to bring all one's loved ones and friends to a reception, following the service.

So one welcomes vast numbers of strangers, many coming for the first time in their lives into your church. They all head for the first rows, thinking to get the best seats, although actually the font is at the back of the church! They are accompanied by lots of little children who quickly commandeer the aisles, sanctuary, or anywhere else that takes their fancy! All this to the background of excited chattering, which in itself is dwarfed by the crying baby whose temper in such a small frame is frightening. And lest we forget, the parents: Mother concerned only that the baby's dress is immaculate; Father keeps testing the camera flash light to make sure that all is in order; the Godparents (chosen not because of their piety, but rather for the extent of their bank balance) look very uncomfortable, not having a clue about what they are there for or what they have to do or say; the remainder of those present impatiently waiting for the reception so they can wet the baby's head. I hope that by now the reader has got the picture.

Regular members of the congregation can be a little bit resentful if their usual place is occupied by a total stranger! 'Why can't we have baptisms on the fifth Sunday of the month, or at a private service?' is their demand. The fact that Grandmother has just

45

flown in and is only here for the weekend cuts no ice with any of them. Gritting his teeth, the chaplain continues the service to the bitter end, shaking hands at the end of the service with those he knows will never be seen again, including the father, who volunteers, 'How much do I owe you?' whilst jingling coins in his trouser pocket! A look of relief as I tell him that baptisms are for free! At this stage, my mind turns to colleagues who take a different stance when dealing with such cases:

'We only have baptisms on the fourth Sunday of the month,' or, 'Are you on the electoral role? If not then I'm sorry!' or 'You will have to attend for three Sundays before the service and then again afterwards to receive your certificate.'

Whilst I respect such views, in fact possibly admire them, it is the baby who suffers. Jesus said, 'Suffer the little children to come to Me.' So I stick to my guns, knowing that I shall probably never see any of them again. But, praise the Lord, sometimes I am proved wrong and get my just reward.

On one occasion the telephone disrupted my lunch (as usual) with an enquiry similar to those I have mentioned above, but with a difference.

'I have already enquired with two vicars who declined to take the service,' (for one of the reasons given above), he said, but then (surely the unkindest cut of all) 'one of them gave me your number saying you may be able to help.'

Help I did, but with results I didn't dare to hope for. It was a small party who were polite, well behaved and listened intensely to everything I said. The baptism itself was meaningful, the baby perfectly behaved and the service appreciated. After the service, the father approached me with a generous donation and then said, 'I was very moved by the service, so would you please baptise me as well?'

After lessons and instructions, baptised he was and he proved to be a faithful Christian. As for me, I gave thanks – two for the price of one! Praise the Lord! Two souls who have become the children of God, washed in the blood of the lamb and blessed by the gift of the Holy Spirit.

THE TWO SIDES OF MINISTRY

In May 1989, I wrote:

Following this 'Vicar Writes', you will find my annual report to be presented next Sunday. As you would expect, it includes details about church worship, activities of parishioners, about ordinary decent people going about church business seeking the will of Almighty God, and it reflects the life of St Mary's as a respected and revered institution.

But there is another side of life at Rotterdam, which, whilst St Mary's is not actually part of it, is there and goes on. This other side of life is shady, immoral, frightening and dangerous. It includes prostitution, drugs and drink abuse. It is even to do with murder.

It is a side of life with which, as an active priest, I have on occasions been inevitably involved, both as chaplain to St Mary's and as the padre to the Missions to Seamen. Heads and tails (if you think about it) are the opposite ends of the spectrum. Heads includes visiting good people in their spotless homes, or in hospital wards; carrying the reserved sacrament; sharing in fellowship with other Christians, working towards successful Christian stewardship, through meetings and with individual members of St Mary's, or with mission staff; enjoying a real sense of fellowship with likeminded people; being part of the body of Christ.

In complete contrast is the other side of the coin: engaging with unpleasant characters in unsavoury places; trying to unravel the truth from someone who has completely forgotten what it is like to speak the truth; visiting prisoners in their cells, as opposed to patients in hospital wards; experiencing a frightening sense of danger in threatening circumstances, including the fear of being sucked into the mire by which you are surrounded. One of the biggest problems in all sorts of counselling is getting to the truth. The number of times I have said to someone I am trying to help, 'If you had a pain in your head and you went to a doctor and told him you had a pain in your foot, you should not be surprised if he failed to heal you. If you really want to get out of this mess and you want me to help you then you must tell me the truth, the whole truth, and nothing but the truth. Warts and all.'

Yet it is not all gloom and doom. There is honour amongst thieves; people who are down and out do try and help each other out. Adversity may make strange bedfellows, but in most cases, having made their bed, they are prepared to lie on it. But that is not all. In the dingiest and darkest corners, there is always some light, a glimmer of hope in the most sordid of situations. So suddenly and unexpectedly, a little act of kindness or compassion suddenly breaks through, like the sun's fleeting appearance in the midst of a cloudy sky. There is so much good in the worst of us and so much bad in the best of us. And that is why Christ was such a wonderful Saviour. He embraced both sides of the coin. So he said to his disciples, 'Come unto me all that travail and heavy laden, and I will refresh you.' He also said, 'So God loved the world – that if any man sin, we have an advocate with the Father, and he is the propitiation for our sins.'

Compare the human equivalent: 'Lock him up and throw away the key!' to what Jesus said to the dying thief on the cross: 'Today thou shalt be with me in paradise.' Negative sentiments ignore the fact that for every person locked up inside there are up to ten loved ones outside – innocent women, children and more often than one would think, men.

I feel terribly privileged that throughout my ministry in Rotterdam (both within St Mary's and the Missions to Seamen) I have been heavily involved in both sides of the coin. I am also incredibly grateful that St Mary's has provided me with support, both in sacraments and prayer, enabling me to fulfil both sides of my ministry. Arising from all this I am certain that one of the most necessary assets of a priest is a sense of humour!

HOLY COMMUNION AT SCHIEDAM

Around the same time, I wrote:

On Sunday the 19th, when I reached Schiedam Mission for the evening communion service, the club was really humming. It was alive with the sound of table tennis balls, pool and darts. The television and the jukebox were also competing with each other, to say nothing of the electronic game making such noises that only such machines can make. The music was turned off after I had talked to some of the men. Then followed the ringing of the church bell and then, in comparative silence, I welcomed everyone at the club and invited any who wished to attend the upcoming service. As I said the usual prayers in preparation for the communion, I sneaked in an extra plea for a good congregation. I couldn't help but feel a pang of disappointment when I entered the chapel to find it empty. The muffled sound of snooker balls and bats hitting the table tennis balls crept through the still-open door, but that was all. With a deep sigh, the server pulled it to and the service began. After a few minutes, just in fact when I was reading the gospel, the chapel door opened and in walked a seaman. I stopped the service to welcome him and to enquire from where he came.

'Ethiopia,' he replied.

I then asked him if he wished to receive communion, to which he replied in the affirmative. So the service continued to the end. After disrobing I went out to greet my congregation of one, who seemed reluctant to leave his seat, so I joined him. After a few moments, as if by the turning on of a tap, he told me the following:

'I am an Ethiopian and the only Christian on board my ship of thirty-three men. It is wonderful to be able to speak to another Christian and to receive the sacrament.'

As I listened to this outpouring I felt suddenly ashamed, because earlier I had asked myself, 'Was it all worthwhile for just one seaman?' I then recalled the text, 'Where two or three are gathered together in my name, there am I in the midst of them.' I also recalled Philip being sent to the desert, finding and baptising the first Ethiopian into the church, and my evening became complete.

FATHER FORGIVE

In May 1995, I wrote:

Although he smiled up at me bravely, the pain and distress were obvious. And no wonder! He had been stabbed no less than seven times by a fifteen-year-old boy bent on stealing Df1,400 from his shop till. It was not only his pain that was obvious, but his wife's too, whom I had just driven to the hospital. Her anguish and shock were tangible and added to the horror of the situation. But that's not all. We left two bewildered and frightened children behind in the flat above the shop, who had been sucked up into the atmosphere surrounding the terrible incident.

Where are we going so wrong, I agonised, that a fifteen-year-old child could strike a man in the throat and then when he falls to the ground, stab him six more times? It is not enough to say, 'How awful, but thank God that will never happen to me!' because I am writing about a family who are part of our worshipping community at St Mary's.

Another family that I am visiting at this time are grieving that their sixteen-year-old son, still at school, has left home against his parents' wishes and is living in an awful bedsit, sleeping with a woman. Is not the problem that discipline is now an ugly word? Authority is being whittled away from the police, teachers and parents too. The current liberating trend is making old values harder to maintain. The hour of arriving home for teenagers is being extended and it is very difficult to swim against the tide – 'All my friends can stay out late, so why can't I?

But the tragedies that are happening, even within the small confines of St Mary's, bring home the awfulness and seriousness of the situation. It is still true that on occasions one has to be cruel to be kind. Furthermore, those children who do not want to be sucked into the prevalent trends desperately need parental support and discipline to maintain standards that they instinctively know to be right. Please pray for these two families (for obvious reasons I am not giving their names). If you have teenage children yourselves then re-examine your relationship with them at this time. The parents of that fifteen-year-old boy, who could end up on a murder charge, and of the sixteen-year-old who could be contracting AIDS even as I write, were ordinary families, now struck down into a living hell. Thank God, therefore, that we Christians can comfort those in such dire distress by reminding them of the words that fell from the master's lips – Father forgive.

FAITH

In November 1987, I was going through a particularly bad patch. Apart from problems connected with my work, I was finding it increasingly difficult to cope with my personal problems. It is perhaps no wonder that my faith was severely tested. So I put pen to paper and wrote about it:

As I struggled with my faith and was meditating on it early one morning, I suddenly came to see that faith was not something that was an obstacle but a wonderful gift. It is faith that allows one to be strong in the most difficult of circumstances, that overcomes barriers and is sometimes the only asset that prevents one from falling from grace, that allows doors to open so that Christ can come in, that permits the grace of the Holy Spirit to move across the face of the waters, unlocking doors and allowing light to enter in. It is faith that allows the words of Christ to enter into the darkest of moments. 'God so loved the world that he gave...' 'Come unto me all that travail. Look at my hands and see the imprints of the nails.'

It is faith that turns darkness into light, sadness into joy, strength sweeping away weakness, but at the same time being aware that our weakness can allow Christ to shine forth in all His glory, to feast on the words of the saints.

'For I am persuaded that neither death or life, nor angels nor principalities, nor powers, nor things present, nor things to come, nor height, nor depth nor any other creature, shall be able to separate us from the love of God, which is in Christ Jesus our Lord.'

No wonder I arose from that meditation renewed and uplifted, and able to successfully put behind me all that hindered the onward march to that place where there is no more sorrow or crying, or any pain, because these former things have passed away. That place where God in all His glory reigned supreme with us, his children, sharing in that paradise that we call heaven.

APPROACHING THE END

In May 1989, which means that I had been in Rotterdam for over five years and was entering the last year of my contract, I remember reflecting on my ministry, both with the Missions to Seamen and St Mary's. During that time I wrote over sixty 'Vicar Writes' and most of them concerned my ministry in Rotterdam. I do hope the few I have reproduced here give an insight of that ministry. I also trust that they make clear that a priest's ministry is like an iceberg, nine-tenths of which is hidden beneath the sea. But I hope it is also clear that so many incidents in which I was involved were of a social or practical nature, which, whilst rewarding, didn't satisfy my longing to be more and more engaged in a spiritual parish ministry. As my time for departure drew ever nearer, I struggled more and more with the question of whether to continue with the mission or seek a more spiritual ministry through parish work. I have often said that if the Good Lord doesn't give then He sends. But this time it wasn't a lady golfer but my son Michael who influenced me. During a visit to us in Rotterdam, he said to me, 'Father, it's time you came home. We want you to be a loving grandfather to our children and to be an integral part of our growing families.'

A quick calculation from 1953 (Hong Kong) to 1988 (The Netherlands) meant that I had been overseas for over thirty-five years! An even quicker reaction brought forward an immediate response.

'Michael,' I said, 'you are absolutely right. I'm coming home.' So there and then I told the mission that at the end of my extended contract my will was to return to pastoral ministry in the UK. This would be a huge wrench for me, as it was attending services at the mission in Cardiff during in my national service that I first became serious about my faith. It was whilst working at the mission that I studied and passed my lay reader exam and then joined the society. It was at the mission in Hong Kong that I knew for certain I wanted

My farewell party, Rotterdam, 1989.

to be a priest. And it was only because the mission employed me as a reader at Newport during holidays from College that I was able to continue supporting my wife and children and continue at St Michael's Theological College where I eventually became ordained.

So I came to an end of my ministry with the mission in the Netherlands. The sadness of leaving behind so many friends and, as in any ministry, the realisation that there was still so much to be done were compensated by my longing to become spiritually involved in the ministry that followed.

In closing *A Man with a Mission*, I printed a variety of letters referring to my work. Similar letters have continued throughout my ministry, but on the whole they are much more personal, such as thanking me for taking weddings, baptisms, funerals and other special services. They were sent to me personally, so are not really suitable for reproducing. However, one letter I would like to share with you was sent to the organiser of my farewell service at Rotterdam. Anton Jansen was an ex-committee member from Dar es Salaam. He remained a good friend and kept in touch through the years, which is why he received an invitation to my retirement service. The following letter was his response.

Unfortunately we cannot attend the retirement service for our good friend John Taylor because of a small distance problem. However, for what it is worth, herewith a few memories which may enlighten the proceedings!

We first met John and Rose Taylor when we arrived in Dar es Salaam in 1963 as manager of the local office of Holland Africa Line. The committee of the Missions to Seamen, which met on a monthly basis, existed to keep an eye on the padres to assist him with advice. In fact the monthly meetings were merely occasions to put in writing what had been arranged beforehand. John was always in a hurry so that he could do more. The Mission had very attractive new premises adjacent to the harbour which was only completed in 1956. John was the 'cannonball' and his charming and efficient wife, Rose, kept him in check and ran the books. With two small children, Michael and Elizabeth, she had little spare time.

John's first goal was to get the Archdeacon in Nairobi to agree to serve beer on the mission premises. Sailors were no longer hijacked riffraff from the streets of Liverpool, Amsterdam or Hamburg, but skilled technicians who deserved to enjoy a beer after working hard in extreme humidity on board ships. The fossilised Archdeacon was not going to take risks with a beer licence and kept his foot down. Fortunately he was replaced shortly by the local Bishop John Sepeko, a fine and understanding gentleman. He agreed to the selling of beer.

The next project was a swimming pool and in view of the number of expected guests, it should be of generous proportions. That needed money. And so the well-known John Taylor's annual fete was born. I still see him in his flowing white nightdress strutting through the bazaar, selling advertising to the Indian Duke Wallach's. They were of all religions: Hindus (various castes) and Muslims also of many denominations. They liked this Mongo (Swahili for Christian or white man) who took the trouble to visit them personally in their shops.

To help with the bazaar, John organised various expatriate nationalities into groups: the Dutch complete with windmill; a German Oompah band and sausages; Irish dancers, etc., etc. The events became so popular the pool was built and paid for in no time. The ships in port also donated generously towards the cost. And the monthly magazine flourished with more and more advertisements.

He realised that sailors, more than anything else, missed their wives and children. He fixed that one by opening the mission to membership by local expatriate families who were only too happy to use the pool together with their young children. Mind you, eighteen-year-old Miss Dar es Salaam was also considered and accepted. All this made the sailors feel at home, which was of course the object of the exercise.

I could go on.

Anton Jansen

A LETTER FROM BRIAN

Moving from the past to the present, I have also received many letters of appreciation for my book. One such letter sums up most of the others. I print it here in full. Why? Because it confirms my ambition that through its pages God may be seen at work. I cannot ask for anything more.

Dear John,
I am really enjoying 'A Man with a Mission'. The stories you tell are a roller coaster of fun, sadness, irony and drama. Your determination and courage are very inspiring indeed. Given that I've spent most of my life being anti-religious it is a rare treat to have discovered your life quite by chance. I can almost hear you saying 'God sends' right now.

I do hope I get the opportunity to thank you in person. Your book has inspired me to get off my backside and get involved in helping folks in my community. I cannot pay you a greater compliment.
  Brian

A letter from the Archbishop of Canterbury

Lambeth Palace London SE1 7JU

18th April 1988

Dear John,

    I am delighted that you are to be instituted at St. Margaret's at the end of this week.

    (Your letter has been rather buried in the Pending tray) but I will put you down for our prayers on Friday and hope you have as much joy as that delectable parish sounds capable of yielding. I envy you.

    With love to you and Adrienne,

        Yours ever,

The Rev. Canon J.R. Taylor,
The Vicarage,
Warnham,
Horsham,
West Sussex.

At the beginning of this exercise I intended to produce only a few copies for family and closest friends. However, due to the support and encouragement I have received, I have decided to print 500 copies.

The Parish Church of St Margaret's Warnham

Before I share with you my wonderful ten years at Warnham, I need to recap briefly for the benefit of those who have not read *A Man with a Mission*. It was during my time of National Service that I first felt drawn to the Church. As my father was an atheist and did his best to indoctrinate us, his children, into the same mould, I had, up to that time, almost no experience of religion or the Church. But like a magnet, the call of service to Almighty God took hold of me and just would not let me go. It became so strong that after demob I resigned my job and joined the Missions to Seamen as a lay assistant. I was posted to Hong Kong and it was there that I finally decided that I wanted to be a priest. The realisation was accompanied by a vision which saw me standing in a vicarage garden looking at the house with roses around the door. Now read on.

On Friday 22nd April 1988, after my induction and institution as vicar of Warnham and as I stood in the vicarage garden, I knew that that moment of vision had arrived. What wasn't in that vision was the village pub, which actually was our next-door neighbour! But to me it completed the picture of what, by the grace of God, I hoped to achieve – the love of God flowing in abundance from the beautiful church of St Margaret's into every house in the village; the village school, the shops, yes and the two pubs as well.

As I stood there, as many incumbents before me had done, I realised that I was but part of a long chain of incumbents, here for a short time, and then the baton would be passed onto my successor. But I had the responsibility and the honour of maintaining its value and its worship. Yes, and its fabric too. An incredible sense of humility swept over me and with it the realisation that (thankfully) it was God's church and not mine.

I gathered together some historical facts which, as well as being awesome, filled me with pride. I share a few of them with you now.

The Industrial Revolution brought wealth to rural Sussex from manufacture and trade, this including Warnham. Churchgoing for the less than faithful still tended to be an obligation and the churches were large enough to accommodate them all. The massive changes brought by the two World Wars impacted hugely on rural churches throughout England. The Church of England regarded its resources of priest and cash as inadequate and with urban demands being accorded higher priority for growing populations, rural parishes have increasingly faced economies, including: amalgamations; sale of clergy houses with or without smaller alternative accommodation; disposal or change of use of redundant churches; exhaustive (or should that be exhausting?) use of retired clergy and priests in lay employment doing church work in their spare time. Warnham Rectory was sold early in the twentieth century. The present vicarage, although much smaller, is nevertheless a very pleasant four-bedroom house. And for the record, I have retired (or attempted to) three times!

SOME INTERESTING HISTORY

My research of Warnham's history revealed that it celebrated its 700th birthday in 1947, the parish having been created and its first Vicar appointed, Robert De Dorking, on the 18th July 1247. An old map shows the church began as a shrine in the Wealden Forest, standing at the crossroads of two very ancient tracks, both of which are still present today.

The oldest part of the present building is fourteenth century and includes the north wall and the Carryall Chapel. The tower is early sixteenth century and carries a peal of ten bells (the last two being added during my incumbency). The bell tower is ascended by a ladder, dated, in rough-cut figures, 1669.

The font is early Norman. At the east end of the north aisle is the Carlyle Chapel, built about 1480 by John Carlyle, sergeant-at-law. On the north wall of the chapel is a monument to Sir John Carlyle and his family, erected in 1613. At the east end of the south aisle is the chapel of our Lady of Pity (now used as a vestry) built by Richard Mychal of Field Place, Warnham about 1534. The poet Shelley, whose grandmother was a Mychal, was born at Field Place on 4th August and baptised in Warnham Church on 7th September 1792. Beneath the floor of this chapel are buried members of the Shelley family, including the poet's son, Charles, aged eleven years. The church plate still in use today was presented by Sir Timothy Shelley in 1771.

The Church was extensively restored in 1885 by the generosity of Charles Lucas of Warnham Court. At this time the present sanctuary was built, the porch erected, the yew arch planted outside the west door and the church re-roofed and re-seated. The chandelier under the tower and all the iron work in the church were made at Warnham Blacksmith's Forge in 1886. The registers date from 1558, the first year of the reign of Queen Elizabeth. No wonder then that I felt humbled and awed as I stood in the vicarage garden, but not in despair for I believed that God had called me to serve him in this corner of his vineyard. I also believed that it is by our weakness that God's strength and power are revealed. So I offered up a prayer for his blessing and moved into the vicarage.

SOME INSIDE INFORMATION

Before my induction, I had taken up the offer made by the previous incumbent to join him and his wife for lunch. I was immediately taken with both of them and left in no doubt that theirs was a difficult act to follow! But as readers of my first book will know, up to now I have had many experiences in very different situations and if the truth be known, wasn't expecting anything new to cope with. How wrong can you be? I soon came to see that I was entering what was for me a completely new situation, that of ministering to an 'up and down' village. The squire of the village was Charles Lucas, who lived in Warnham Park, containing a herd of famous deer that were exported all over the world. One can see by the brief history I have shared with you just how important a person he was. Charles was also the local county councillor and the patron of the church, which gave him the right to select the incumbent, which was now me. He was also a member of the PCC; I say member but in fact he was far more. For example, when a topic for debate arose, Charles (I was told) waited till everyone had said their piece then gave his own opinion, which was then adopted. A good example of his influence arose concerning the reciting of the Lord's Prayer. I noticed that a modern new version of it was used at most services, but not when the Lucas family was present. Charles didn't like it, so the old version was used instead. This was a great shock to me and totally unacceptable.

The previous incumbent enlightened me about a ritual he had inherited. An invitation to lunch would appear, which was a command performance in fact. Lunch was always very pleasant until around the sweet time when Charles would raise a point about some aspect of church procedure of which he didn't approve. The version of the Lord's Prayer being used was a good example. I decided that instead of being summoned, I would invite him first for coffee and then raise any topic with which I was concerned. With the two versions used of the Lord's Prayer, depending whether or not he was in church, I pointed out that it was the vicar and warden's responsibility and not just his alone. He was rather taken aback by this approach, although I must say he didn't try and fight it. In fact he was very gracious. From then on only one version was used!

For the record, I still enjoyed many excellent lunches with the Lucas family, but without reference to church affairs, which were dealt with at the proper place and time, during council meetings. In fact Charles and Thelma became very good friends and I still keep in touch with Thelma today.

Until a few years ago, when the Lucas family came to church, they arrived in up to three Rolls Royces, all parked outside the church. They went to their allotted pews, with places reserved for the drivers at the back of the church. This was no longer the case, but it does help to understand the power and authority he wielded in all aspects of church life.

The village itself had its own upstairs and downstairs division. Many of the houses in the village once belonged to the Lucas family and some still do. The rest of the village lived in the small council estate and if the truth be known, were considered by some to be second-rate citizens! The saving grace, however, was that it was Charles himself who first pointed out to me the divide and urged me to do everything possible to close the gap. The division could most clearly be seen in the attendance at the village school. Most of the church school children came from the council estate, children from the rest of the village usually went to private schools.

The upstairs and downstairs nature of Warnham can be seen in its history also. Famous names and people emerge as one looks back, all of whom have played an important part in shaping the destiny of the village: none more than the Shelley family, who lived at Field Place on the edge of the village. It was here that Shelley was born. His early schooling was given by the local vicar. He then went on to Eton and Oxford University. Unfortunately his work, 'The Necessity of Atheism', gave such offence that he was sent down. He quarrelled bitterly with his father and from then on led a wandering life. In 1816 he left England never to return. He settled in Italy, where some of his most famous works were written, and it was here that he became friends with Lord Byron. Shelley was considered to be a radical and extremist; his revolutionary views were not acceptable to members of his own class, although his poetry and political writing became very important in the Chartist and early labour movement in Britain, which he did not live to see. What a pity he did not stay in England to write on the natural beauties of Sussex. His poem 'The Question' may be a celebration of the Field Place estate and a lament for his exile from it and his family. In it he wrote, 'It might make one in love with death, to think that one should be buried in so sweet a place.'

In 1822, he was drowned while returning in a sailing boat to his home in Spezia Bay. His widow, Mary, did not like Field Place as she considered it damp, so it was leased to various tenants and finally sold off in 1929 (the year I was born!). Dead he might be but his name lives on in the Horsham Shelley Festival Committee, an active group that visit his old home and promote his work and writings.

However, from the ranks of the downstairs also emerge people and groups who have added to Warnham's richness. Shelley became known worldwide; equally well known in Warnham was one Michael Turner who was for many years church clerk and sexton. He was well known for his musical accomplishments and led the choir for many years. A glass cabinet in the church contains his viol, tuning fork, music books and his spectacles. He is buried in the churchyard with the following inscription on his gravestone:

His duty done beneath this stone,
Old Michael lies at rest,
His rustic rig, his song, his jig,
Were ever of the best.
With nodding head, the choir he led
That none should sing too soon
The second too, He sang full true
His viol played the tune.
And when at last his age had passed
One hundred less eleven
With faithful cling to fiddle string
He sang himself to heaven.

There were others too whose names are honoured in the history books and surprisingly, considering the size of Warnham, there were three who played cricket for Surrey and England.

THE COCKERELS

Warnham had at one time a strange religious sect known as the Cockerels. Their faith was very similar to that practised by the Quakers, although the prominence of St Margaret's Church was never challenged. They were registered as 'Dependents Depend on God'. Not surprisingly, with such a title, many villagers considered them rather aloof and distant. Nevertheless, they were respected both in business and in their dedication to their faith and worship. Very little is known of their teaching as they took little or no part in the activities of the village. No effort was made to bring others into their circle, but any who did were made welcome. They originally met in people's houses, but in 1874 a chapel was built by the brothers at a cost of £150. At its first meeting a hymn was sung followed by prayer, followed by a speaker after which anyone present was allowed to give a testimony on a subject of their own choosing. This could be about their health, friends, problems or indeed anything. They also met on Tuesday and Thursday evenings. At these meetings it was customary to serve a hot cup of cocoa, from which the name Cockerels evolved. Their business in the village was known as 'Linfield, Luff and Co', which soon became 'Warnham Stores'. Items were marked

The Cockerels attending a funeral.

63

with farthings (e.g. penny three farthings) and to level out the price, a packet of pins was given as change.

The cockerels were easily recognised in the accepted habits of their sect. The men wore dark suits with narrow trousers and jackets tailored to exclude any collars or lapels. The women dressed in long black skirts and black tops with bonnets tied under their chins.

They were thrifty themselves but generous in helping others. It was generally thought in the village that the more devout Cockerels did not approve of marriage or children, which is why they probably failed to continue as a sect, although there are still some survivors of the Warnham Dependents today.

There was a small chapel congregation, but with a strong Sunday school (possibly because its faithful members were treated to an annual seaside outing, one of the highlights of the year). Nevertheless, the church was always at the heart of the village and still is to this day. The more I learnt about Warnham's history, the prouder I became of being the thirty-seventh vicar of the parish. Although the names of all the thirty-six vicars in the church are recorded, none of them appear to be valued especially as part of its general history. My name has now been added to the list and I expect to receive the same fate! But this only enhances what I wrote a few pages ago, that the incumbent is merely a caretaker during his incumbency; the church belongs to its parishioners. Vicars were, however, widely respected and this included their wives. Until fairly recently, if a child met the vicar's wife he or she had to curtsy or bow to her. Sometimes they tried to avoid this, but inevitably they were seen and reported. This led to a caning at school and further punishment when they arrived home.

ALE HOUSES

Before leaving the history of Warnham, I must say something about the inns, ale houses and smuggling. Apart from The Sussex Oak (my next-door neighbour) and the Greets Inn (both of which are in operation today), there were a few other ale houses. Warnham geography could explain why it was always considered a favourite haunt of smugglers. It had easy access to dense woodlands and could have been a regular route to the coast, hence the many tunnels that linked The Greets Inn with others. It is a fact that many land owners were happy to stock their cellars with the finest wines and spirits from the continent without querying their source. Warnham also had one or two windmills, which were also frequently used to hide contraband. Warnham then, although only a small village, has an interesting history. Lying not far from Horsham, it is considered a very pleasant place to live and the cost of its houses reflects this fact.

To return to the present time, the financial aspects of living in Warnham were a shock. Being in the mission field meant a fairly small stipend, but everything was provided for; the accommodation was complete with furniture whilst the car belonged to the mission, including its running costs. This was not the case with an incumbent in an English parish. The house is provided, but not its furnishings. The rates are paid for but that's all. The car and its running is the responsibility of the vicar. Imagine my amazement, therefore, when I entered the vicarage for the first time. To quote the well-known fairy tale, 'Mother Hubbard's cupboard was bare.' Gone were the carpets, the curtains, the cooker, freezer and washing machine, the lamp shades and even some of the light bulbs. The previous incumbent was within his rights in taking what he did, but it left me with an almost insolvable financial situation. Being in the mission field for over thirty years, plus putting our children through public schools, had been a struggle, leaving only a very small bank balance, nothing near enough to purchase a car and furnish the vicarage.

My family have heard me say times without number, 'If the Lord doesn't give, He sends.' This had been my experience throughout my ministry, but even I struggled to believe what happened as I prepared to take up residence at Warnham.

HELP FROM BISHOP JOHN POOLE HUGHES

As mentioned in my first book, Bishop John Hughes was a dear and very close friend. I first met him at Theological College when he was chaplain. Round about the same time as I went to Dar es Salaam, as chaplain, he was appointed as Bishop of South West Tanganyika. Whenever he came down to Dar, I met with him and sometimes put him up. We used to say the offices together as, although a very dear friend, he was also my Father in God. It was, for example, to him I went when asked to be archdeacon, seeking his advice, which was as always wise and to the point. Later he returned to the UK and was appointed Bishop of Llandaff. Whenever I was in the UK I tried to see him and (roles reversed) I sometimes stayed with him in his residence.

I last went to see him about a month before I was due to be appointed Vicar of Warnham and, as usual, we said evensong together. Afterwards I made my excuses to leave as I had another anointment pending, but he said, 'Sit down, John, I want to talk to you.'

I sat down. He questioned me about Warnham, including the cost of moving and settling in. He then asked me if I had a car, to which the answer was no. Then, to my amazement, he dropped some car keys on the table.

'I won't be using my car much longer,' he said. Sadly he was in the advanced stages of cancer. 'Please accept them with my love.'

I was overwhelmed and tried to express my thanks, but failed miserably. I was driving a borrowed car from a friend in Cardiff who quickly came to take it away, whilst I, still trying to take in what had just happened, said my goodbyes and drove away in my very own brand new car. Sadly, John died very shortly afterwards, although his precious memory will live on as long as I live. Readers of my first book will recall that when I left Theological College he gave me a cheque for £500, which was a Godsend at that time. Now his car, which meant that the amount required to move into Warnham was nearly halved. It gave me great pleasure incidentally when, many years later, I was able to send £500 back to his diocese of South West Tanganyika.

HELP FROM A PUBLICAN

A friend of a friend who was managing director of a brewery had recently refurnished his house when his company offered to do the same. He pointed out that he had only just done so, but the reply came back (it was something to do with income tax) that this was the only way the bonus could be given. When he heard of my dilemma, he offered all that was being renewed to me for £200. This included carpets and curtains, a dining room suite and kitchen table and chairs, also two bedroom suites. The icing on the cake was when another friend offered to and indeed did pay all the removal charges. Other friends offered various bits and pieces, filling all the gaps.

Due to people's generosity, the winning post was now in sight. In fact all that was now missing to complete the jigsaw was the equipment for the kitchen. I knew I had to provide these items, but this was only possible if I took out a loan of £2,500, which I did. Writing this now it is hard to believe, but the very next day, and to my complete surprise, came a cheque for £2,500: a gift from the mission to express thanks for my long service.

So my mission, which seemed financially impossible, became very possible and unbelievably I was able to move into the vicarage at Warnham with everything new and no overdraft. No wonder my favourite saying is, 'If the Lord doesn't give, He sends.'

Finally, whilst writing about gifts, I must mention some that didn't come from God, but from parishioners. Sometimes a knock on the door heralded items from parishioners' gardens. On other occasions, whilst leaving the vicarage, one found a parcel of goodies left on the doorstep. In Dar es Salaam I used to say that if all the gifts for the building of the mission were to be returned to the ships stores, the mission would collapse like a pack of cards! I couldn't quite say the same thing about Warnham, but the similarity was nevertheless there.

GETTING THE SHOW ON THE ROAD

Before I could start planning for the future there were two items that needed my immediate attention. The first was the baptisms that had piled up during the interregnum. Interviews, teaching and the baptisms themselves took considerable time and effort and as a result, some six months passed before I had cleared the backlog and could turn my attention to the second problem, which proved far more difficult to solve.

The village had its fair share of teenagers who, because there was no place where they could legitimately meet, congregated at various points in the village, all of which proved unpopular with adults, so they were constantly being moved on. Their present meeting point was right outside the church! Not that they did any harm as such, but twelve to fifteen teenagers blocked up all the pavement and furthermore frightened some of the older folk who had to pass through them on their way to the village shop, next to the church. Inevitably they were noisy and being full of youthful energy, indulged in a fair amount of horseplay, which added to the problem. Furthermore, they were 'cheesed off' with being continually moved on from pillar to post. I arranged a meeting with them, which proved to be most helpful, and I promised to try and solve the problem. I had learnt of a large caravan that was no longer used by its owner, who would actually be pleased to be rid of it. I then found a little waste ground, not too close to any houses, where I could (with permission from the village committee) house the caravan. Even more encouragingly, I collected the names of five responsible adults who would be prepared to supervise its use when it would be open in the evenings for the teenagers.

I requested and received permission to address the council, but it unfortunately ended in failure. My address was not helped when a person receiving counselling from me burst into the hall just as I was about to speak and started screaming at me about something I hadn't done. Eventually, hospitalisation was needed for her, but in the meantime my request for provision of a temporary unit where the youth could meet was turned down. So the problem remained. However, I am pleased to say that as a result of the stewardship campaign, emphasising the use of time, talents and money, the original potential helpers started a youth club in the village hall.

Within a few months I felt I had found my feet. I had a general layout of the village and a good idea of the strengths and weaknesses in the parish. I was so thankful that the worship and church attendance was acceptable (although I obviously prayed that it would in time grow). The main weakness was the unsatisfactory state of the finances, which needed immediate strengthening. Like it or not then, at the top of the agenda was the need to improve the finances of the parish. Each church has a diocesan quota to meet in addition to the normal expenses of the parish and in this St Margaret's failed. The old system of the Vicar sitting outside the church or in the porch at a time of crisis with cap in hand waiting for donations just didn't work anymore! Furthermore, the parish had previously depended on the generosity of the Lucas Family to a large extent. They had, for example, only recently paid for a new organ. But, as Charles told me, they could no longer bail out the church when it was in need. My mind went back to Dar es Salaam days at the time of Tanzania's Independence. The Lutheran Church was well placed, but only because of its financial reliance on Germany. The elders then made a brave and bold decision; they would no longer rely on help from abroad, but would become financially independent themselves. Despite fears from some, the drive towards independence proved a success. If the Lutheran Church in Tanzania could do it, I determined that we could – and without relying on one family's generosity. So after meticulous planning we launched a Christian stewardship campaign.

CHRISTIAN STEWARDSHIP

Christian stewardship recognises that everything we have is a gift from God; therefore, we should give a due portion back to him, not only in money but in time and talents also. The name for the scheme is TRIO.

This immediately presents an entirely different scenario. First of all it challenges the individual to seriously consider his or her financial commitment rather than merely looking at the loose change in one's pocket at collection time. Secondly it asks the question, what talents do I have that can be used instead of paying someone else to do the same work? Third is the consideration of how much time an individual can give in helping to build up the body of the church by joining working parties or committees, like the PCC or a fundraising group.

Pledging commitment enables the treasurer to have an accurate assessment of the finances of the parish, rather than the hit or miss situation that existed before. And so a stewardship campaign was set in motion. For the record I must state that the parish had launched a stewardship campaign a few years earlier, but with only limited success. Many parishes enter into such a scheme as a one-off venture. But that never has the desired effect. It needs to be a continuous project, so newcomers can enter into the scheme and those in it are reminded of their commitment and encouraged to review their promise from time to time. I determined to ignore these pitfalls and by the grace of Almighty God, we succeeded.

First of all I gathered together those whom I thought would give wholeheartedly to the scheme. I pointed out that unless they were prepared to pledge themselves, they couldn't expect others to make a commitment. All but three agreed, which left me with eight souls to form the committee. The campaign then followed the usual pattern and was a resounding success. The giving doubled, some wonderful talents were unearthed and enthusiastic new committees formed. Far harder to achieve was the acceptance that one-tenth of our total income should be given to away to charities. More common was that charities could only be considered after all parish commitments had been met. I am pleased to say that, through stewardship, both those goals were achieved.

Apart from planned giving, we also held various fundraising events, the largest of which were fetes. Apart from the money raised, involvement by those outside the core of regular worshippers was tremendously important and often resulted in an increase in the number of regular worshippers as well.

Renewed energy ensured that the traditional fundraising schemes, such as coffee mornings, jumble sales and raffles, made an important contribution to the finances of the parish.

In addition to all this, I have always found that having a project in hand keeps everyone on their toes as there is always something ahead to strive for. It keeps the kettle on the boil. The first was to make the parish financially viable; the second was to renew the roof, which was showing urgent need of repair.

They say that time and tide wait for no man; it is also true that the best plans of men go astray. My long-time priorities remained, although they were kicked out of touch when something new cropped up and it became priority number one. I have always believed and practised that people come before things, but in that mysterious way that the Lord works, his wonders to perform, this new challenge presented an opportunity for the village as a whole to unite in a charitable act. And so it proved. Both the upstairs and the downstairs in the village responded magnificently

LAURA SOMMERFORD

Let me explain. Laura lived with her parents in the village council estate. Since the day she was born, on 10th October 1986, she had suffered the effects of cerebral palsy, leaving her brain damaged and unable to walk due to pelvic tilt. It was not until her father, Jim, saw a walker advertised in a magazine in 1992 that he realised this could possibly help his daughter to walk independently. The contraption would enable Laura to stand upright and would be fitted to her legs. She would be lifted onto the frame, with the help of a pivot at the back, enabling her to turn corners instead of just walking in straight lines. The cost of the contraption, plus other expenses, came to around £2,000. Jim had been saving to try and reach this figure and had raised about £500 when a letter from the manufacturers informed him that the cost of obtaining the walker had gone up by £500. He was back to square one. My experience as Archdeacon in Tanzania (the eyes and ears of the bishop) helped me to hear of this tragedy from a neighbour who was my eyes and ears for that part of the council estate, and an immediate visit confirmed what I had been told. It was around mid-

November and the news had spoilt any hopes of a happy Christmas for the Sommerford family. I told them not to despair as something would turn up (I had already decided in my own mind that by hook or by crook the money could be found, and quickly too). The December magazine was actually late for the printers, awaiting my 'Vicar Writes'. I had already decided my theme for the magazine, but I pushed that aside because I saw it as a golden opportunity to get help for Laura. Hence my Christmas letter, headed:

A Very Special Christmas Present for Laura!

In it I gave a very brief account of Laura's background and the disappointing news that the cost of the walker had increased by the money they had managed to save. I had calculated that the total cost would be in the region of £2,000. I informed my readers that I was so certain the money would be forthcoming that I had already ordered a walker and booked the hotel in Manchester where the family could

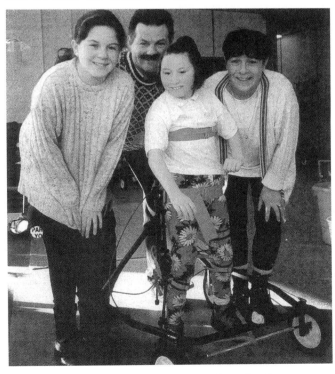

Laura Sommerford with her family and walker.

stay whilst the walker would be fitted, so they would be back home before Christmas. The result was amazing. Within hours of the magazine reaching its readers £3,500 in cheques or cash came through the vicarage letter box. In the end there was enough to pay for the walker and a lift to be fitted to their car as well.

But the most amazing thing of all was Christmas morning. The church was packed, including the Sommerford family, complete with Laura and walker at the back of the church. At a suitable time in the service I said, 'Laura, there is a Christmas present for you on the Christmas tree. Would you please come and fetch it? After what seemed an age, Laura left her pew and walked slowly but purposefully down the aisle. Every eye was fixed on her and as she neared the front of the church those same eyes became filled with tears. Claps were turned into cheers as Laura received her present and slowly made her return journey back to her pew. To add to the occasion, the parents had festooned the walker with Christmas decorations. Laura had a sister who came out to help her for the last few steps. She also received a present. But the icing on the cake, as far as I was concerned, came shortly afterwards when, in a simple but deeply profound service, I baptised Laura in the name of the Father and of the Son and of the Holy Ghost, purified in the blood of the lamb, so becoming a child of God and an inheritor of the kingdom of Heaven. She understood, as I signed her with the sign of the cross, that it was an indelible mark of a Christian.

Laura was a pupil of Chailey School, an amazing establishment for seriously handicapped children, which was not far from the parish. It was not surprising, therefore, that I was invited to take assemblies for the children, which of course included Laura. She was always waiting to greet me and proudly made the sign of the cross on her forehead as I came into view. Taking assemblies for these children was a real challenge as their concentration time was severely limited, but the reception I received on arrival and the farewells when I left was sufficient proof to me of the power of the Holy Spirit alive in both the children and the staff, an inspiration to behold. Just in case any reader is asking, 'Why is Canon John taking services in another's parish?' there is a simple explanation. The Vicar of Chailey was blind, so understandably found it too emotionally difficult to cope. I was only too happy to help out.

WARNHAM COURT BOARDING SCHOOL

A similar challenge arose over my ministry at Warnham Court School, run by the London Borough of Lambeth, whose boarders had all received abuse of one kind or another. The atmosphere was entirely different from the village school with very strict control over the pupils who, as a result of their abuse, had been mentally or physically scarred. The first thing I noticed was the dress of the staff, which was extremely casual. The headmaster explained that the children had probably never seen anyone dressed in a suit, which would have immediately put them off. Apart from taking a weekly assembly, I also used to have lunch with the students, which was rather like sitting on an un-exploded bomb. The slightest thing would cause the table to erupt; food would be thrown over the floor and general chaos ensued. As quick as lightning one or more of the staff would come in with a heavy hand, remove the culprit and restore some form of order. I used to feel terrible, but was assured by the staff that I was in no way to blame. I also used to attend the general assembly taken by the headmaster and was most impressed by the way he conducted it. I will never forget on one occasion he called two of the boys up onto the stage. He told them that the other children, the staff, Canon John and he were fed up to the back teeth with the fact that they were always fighting each other! He then picked them both up by the scuff of the neck and said, 'Why do you keep fighting each other?' As quick as a flash came back the answer, 'Because we hate each other!' There was no reply to that.

It was a fairly common experience for one or the other of the children to run away from school and it was always a worrying time before they were returned. The patience and sensitivity of the staff was remarkable and I never once saw anything untoward in all the time I was there.

One of the highlights of my ministry at the school was after an open day for ex-pupils, which fell on a Sunday. I had to leave early because I was conducting evensong in the church. To my utter delight and just before the service began, in walked three of the boys, who stayed for the service and joined me afterwards for refreshments in the vicarage. I remember on another occasion, when my assembly hadn't gone as well as I would have liked, feeling a bit depressed. Then one of the staff said to me, 'You'll never know how much these services mean to us and the children. It is the only time we ever hear the Lord's Prayer said at the school.' Another example of the power of God working through the weakness of another.

WARNHAM'S CHURCH PRIMARY SCHOOL

By comparison, my attendance at the Church Primary School in the village (of which I was chairman of governors) was a real joy. Apart from taking assemblies I sometimes had lunch with the children and it always gave me a thrill when different tables signified that they wanted me to join them. I always sat on a tiny chair, which literally brought me down to size! I remember on one occasion the little girl sitting next to me volunteered the information that her father didn't come home last night.

'Oh,' I replied in as non-committal a voice as possible.

Then came, 'My mum said, "I expect he's gone off with his fancy woman."'

'Oh,' I repeated, this time in a slightly less surprised voice.

Back came the little girl, 'but it's all right because he got drunk and spent the night sleeping in our car!' Talk about out of the mouth of babes and sucklings!

As I got to know the school and staff better, however, I began to sense that all was not as right as it should be. I am referring to the head teacher. She tended to make excuses why the pupils couldn't come down to the church for services on special occasions. I was really worried, however, when the bishop came to address the school assembly and she didn't even greet him or thank him for coming.

I queried the previous chair of governess about her faith and he told me that the subject never arose! My raised eyebrows said it all. How could someone not committed to the spiritual wellbeing of the school be appointed as head teacher? Luckily she was dismissed shortly afterwards, for an entirely different reason. The Lord works in a strange way, his wonders to perform.

I came to see that many of the children had problems out of school to cope with, so I made it my business to be as supportive as possible. In fact my interest became a problem; children would knock on the vicarage door and ask, 'Can Canon John come out to play?' This at a time when new regulations were being introduced limiting the contact adults could have with children (one of the saddest introductions made by authorities, as all children need all the love and attention they can get, which applies to adults as well). In the end, at a school assembly, children were told not to ask Canon John to come out and play, but I still cherish to this day files of letters and paintings that children sent me when I was sick.

JOHN AND OLIVE

To divert from my narrative for a few moments. I am writing this exactly one week away from Christmas 2013. For most of us Christmas cards are arriving from all around. For me they came from every quarter of the globe, including the USA, Australia, Africa and the Continent; one also came from Olive Stanford, a lifelong resident and one of the key figures in the village and church at Warnham. Her husband, John, was equally important and was for many years church warden. He owned his own building firm which he used to great effect for the benefit of the church. Sadly he resigned as church warden before I arrived, due to an altercation with my predecessor. It arose over the proposed marriage of their daughter to the choir director, who had been married before. Not only that but one of the ladies in the choir had borne him a son! Warnham being the village that it was, it meant that everyone knew of the scandal. When it was announced that John's daughter was to be married in St Margaret's, uproar exploded throughout the village. The rule in the church at that time was that a divorcee could not be married in church, although there was a special service that allowed for a blessing of marriage. One could understand the incumbent wanting to make an exception for John, as church warden and generous benefactor, and this no doubt influenced his decision to marry them in church. The village, however, would have none of it and as a result, the archdeacon became involved. In the end, the vicar had to bow to the will of the village and marriage was denied. Understandably, John and Olive were most unhappy about the decision, hence John's resignation as warden, plus the vow that he would never enter the church again. Unfortunately he was true to his word and that was the situation I inherited. Olive, however, a wonderful lady, continued to attend church and was a leading authority in the congregation. Her speciality was gardening, so not unsurprisingly she ran the flower rota. Her own presentations were masterful.

I knew that John missed his church, but was still bitter about the events surrounding his daughter's wedding. I made a special effort to woo him back to church and was making progress when John was diagnosed with cancer. He agreed to me taking him sick communion both to his home and the hospice. I thanked God when after taking him the sacrament he finally agreed to 'come home' to church, on leaving the hospice. Unfortunately he never did leave but he died in peace after receiving the last rites.

Now for another piece of history. About fifty years ago, a wealthy villager purchased two houses: one to ensure we had a district nurse in the village, the other to provide a house for a curate. But as time moved on there were no longer district nurses or curates, so the houses were sold and the money put into a fund to help the poor in the village. A committee appointed to administer the fund and influenced by Olive, who was a leading member, decided to build up the fund by not spending it, in case a plane crashed in the village (as Heathrow and Gatwick were not far away). The vicar was automatically chairman of the committee and I sought to alter this resolution. I pointed out that if a plane did crash the fund would be peanuts compared to the cost of such a disaster. I also made the point that they were not using the fund as had been intended. In the end the committee accepted my point of view and I was given a free hand to use it at my discretion for the purpose for which it was intended. The general thought was that the elderly would benefit most, but I found that most were solvent. There were a few families from the estate who had fallen behind in paying bills, but I sat down with those concerned to help them manage their accounts in the future. But the biggest group of those requiring help were single mums, sometimes with two or even three children. For them the fund was a Godsend. I had the satisfaction that the fund was being used in the way it was intended. I sometimes wonder how it is faring today.

Warnham, incidentally, has recently come into the news over the planned new flight routes taken by aircrafts entering and leaving Gatwick. During my time at Warnham we were thankfully spared the noise of planes entering and leaving, as they used a flight route that missed us out, but the new route plan brings Warnham directly into line. The press reported mass objection from the villagers and I am left wondering if and how the fund is being used to fight this new flight plan.

MINISTRY TO THE ELDERLY

I was constantly being reminded of the number of people from the village who were resident in various nursing homes in the vicinity. At any one time there were up to ten such souls and I determined to visit them all. Most were suffering from Alzheimer's disease, which ensured that one never knew how the visit would go! Put simply (which it is not), the memory is badly affected and with its loss often came a change in character or personality. Sadly those affected often became violent or irrational. One never knew how the patient would be, so it required a great deal of patience and compassion to make a satisfactory visit. On one occasion, the patient would be docile and rational. But on other occasions the same patient could be violent and abusive. Little did I know but the experience would stand me in good stead for when I moved to where we are now, St George's Park, where there are three wards for Alzheimer's patients. But more of that later.

I am often asked, incidentally, which has been the most taxing part of my ministry. I have no hesitation in saying prison visiting in Bangkok, Thailand. But that is closely followed by sick visiting and preparing souls for death. And here I must pause to acknowledge the support I received from Father Joe Meir in Thailand and Lay Reader Vincent Phillips in Warnham.

My first book tells a great deal about Father Joe Meir. I would be remiss not to mention Vincent Phillips in this. I inherited him as a lay reader when I moved to Warnham. As I began my ministry as a reader, I had a soft spot for Vin and valued his support tremendously, especially on my monthly visits to those in nursing homes. Not only did he know the locations of the folks we were visiting, but also some background history. Almost without exception, patients would tell me that none of their relatives had visited them, whereas in fact I often met their relatives at the home when I was visiting! As I have already mentioned, the person concerned often had character changes.

To take but one, before her illness Catherine had been a faithful and regular attender at church services. She had been very successful in her career, including being a spy during the Second World War. She was highly intelligent, well read and it was really very sad to see her as she was now. To my intense embarrassment, when visiting her one day, she suddenly made an attempt to relieve me of my trousers! The next time I visited her, she was confined to her room with a gate across her door, as used to keep a small child from leaving its own space. To my surprise, however, after she died, her will revealed she had left me £50! The one and only time I have been so honoured. I used the money to treat Vin to lunch.

If the incumbent inherited a lay reader, as I did, then one had the authority to withdraw his licence. Vin was always afraid that I might do this (he was already in his eighties) but I never did. Sadly he died shortly after I moved from Warnham and his death left a gap that was never filled.

THE NEED FOR A PROJECT

As mentioned before, I believe that every parish should have a project which will enhance and improve the extent of its activities. Sometimes it is obvious, like when I first moved to Warnham and the need to put the parish on a firm financial footing. This was eventually achieved, but only after two stages: the first was the introduction of a stewardship campaign, of the giving of time, talents and money; the second, and even more importantly, was to set up the system that was constantly under review. I knew from my time as archdeacon and chairman of the diocesan financial board of Dar es Salaam that too often a parish had a stewardship campaign, but did not follow it up. Within three years they found themselves back to square one.

To get the parish ship-shape took about five years, approximately one half of my time there. I then started planning for the future, which I first shared with the parish through the monthly 'Vicar Writes'. This is what I wrote:

I Have a Dream!
More than once I am asked, 'After working in some of the major cities of the world – Cardiff, London, Belfast, Victoria, Hong Kong, Dar es Salaam, Tanzania, Bangkok, Thailand, Rotterdam – don't you find it very boring ending up in a small village like Warnham?' The answer is a resounding NO!

In the ministry of the Missions to Seafarers, an attempt is made to provide through its clubs a home from home. So, for example, in Dar es Salaam, at the heart of the club lies the chapel, always open. A resident chaplain (padre) is available to take services and because the ship's crew may be at sea on a Sunday, every day is a Sunday! The mission in Dar boasted a football pitch, tennis courts, a crazy golf course, snooker hall, library, restaurant and bar, lounge and telephones in a quiet spot, so the men could ring home. Almost every facility that they could find where they lived back home was provided for in the mission club. In this way the mission cares for the material, spiritual and intellectual needs of all seafarers, in body, mind or spirit, irrespective of nationality, colour or creed. Working in a parish, it became immediately obvious that while both church and mission cared for the spiritual welfare of its congregation, in Warnham certainly, and in most parishes there was little or no care for the material needs of the parishioners.

But why should it be? There is a small church hall in the grounds, which if extended could become a social centre for the village, where people could gather for fellowship and other activities. The new unit could become the village centre, benefiting old and young. It would create an opportunity for St Margaret's to exercise a total ministry within the parish.

This is my dream. Will you share in my dream?

My dream received a mixed reaction but, nothing daunted, I had plans of the extension provided by a friendly architect. A special meeting was called and when the 'no's outnumbered those in favour, the plan was scrapped. The dream was in part fulfilled, however, by a new appraisal of the potential of the existing small hall. As a consequence, a crib was established, which proved very popular. At the initiative of Stella Collier, a group of non-church people held meetings in the hall on a regular basis. The hall was also used by the Sunday school and, after the main service, coffee was provided for the congregation. A youth club was started, which was held in the village hall.

A disagreement that I did win, however, was over the renewal of the church roof. Every five years a survey by a local architect determined the state of the building and listed in order of priority what needed attention. The survey revealed that the roof of the church was in a bad state of repair and needed immediate attention. The present slate roof had stood for some hundred years. The church treasurer worked for Warnham Brickworks and was able to secure a generous deal to replace the present slate roof. Warnham tiles were brown and although many were in favour, others including me were not. My training as a civil engineer came to the fore as I pointed out that many of the present slate tiles on the roof could be redressed and used again. There would be, however, new tiles needed to replace those worn out. The firm that provided the present roof was no longer in existence and there was thought to be no other source that could supply the necessary tiles. Then I was reliably informed that there was a firm in Cornwall who did and could supply the tiles we needed. A representative from the firm came to Warnham and confirmed this good news. When I return to Warnham I always look up at the grey slate roof and offer a prayer of thanksgiving.

The retiling of the slate roof.

As I approached my sixty-fifth birthday, I thought seriously of retiring. There was a great deal that I wanted to do, including writing my autobiography. I very much wanted to improve my golf, which meant playing far more regularly than at present. I was also aware that because I had spent so much time abroad, I wasn't as close to family and UK friends as I would wish. Charles Lucas, however, had other ideas. He said that there was still lots to be done in the parish and pleaded with me to stay. I did and with hindsight, it was the right decision. The next five years passed happily and furthermore I was able to start on my book. People asked me why it took so long. The answer was simple: people always come before things. On many occasions, time that I had intended to devote to my writing was overtaken by the needs of parishioners.

Now that I am retired I still face the same problem. My ministry at St George's arose when the Vicar of Ditching asked me, whilst still at Streat, to take on a ministry to the patients at St George's (more about that later). From my old parish of Ditchling, Streat and Westmeston, I am called from time to time to take services. And also St John's, Burgess Hill, where we now worship; they all call upon my services from time to time, which I find demanding and time-consuming. But, to be honest, I wouldn't have it any other way.

Because of the shortage of clergy and money to pay them, many parishes are being enlarged, with the consequence that some incumbents have extra churches to look after. The diocese of Chichester has not been affected as much as others; Warnham and Ditchling still only has one church. I have, however, a colleague from the diocese of Lincoln who has seven churches to minister to. And although I didn't know it whilst in Warnham, the axe was to fall on my next two parishes when Streat and Westmeston were united with Ditchling.

Having just one church at Warnham has its pros and cons. If one has more than one church then the vicar can use the same sermon twice! Having three services every Sunday, plus the fact that some parishioners go to two or even all three of them, means that a different address is needed for each! I was lucky to have a lay reader, but in fairness to him (and the congregation), I could only use him sparingly. We also had a Holy Communion service on Thursdays at 11.00 a.m. The congregation consisted mainly of elderly people. I say 11.00 a.m.; in actual fact, it started when all the regular congregation, plus walking sticks or Zimmers, had arrived! I also took sick communion to those unable to get to church. This, plus the services I took at the nursing homes, saints' days and other special occasions, meant a fairly full timetable of services. On one Sunday of the month we held a special children's service. I was extremely fortunate that I had a team of some six parishioners who used to meet with me to plan the service. Because of their contribution, this service became very popular, so much so that visitors from other parishes used to come and see what we did and how we did it, returning home with fresh ideas.

This brings me to one of my hobby horses, namely youth work. There is a general conception that children's church and youth work is for the younger person. If a parish is lucky enough to have a curate, be sure that this work will fall on his hands. Whereas a younger person has certain advantages, an older person has gifts still to offer and, in any case, the incumbent has the cure of all souls and especially children.

Archbishop Carey recently said, 'The Church of England is doomed because it hasn't done enough to bring in the children.' I personally have never found my age a barrier to working with children. Indeed I am thinking (if ever I do finish this second part of my biography) of printing another full of letters, paintings, get well cards, from Thailand, Holland and Warnham, all from children. Not only are they very touching, but they contain a surprising amount of theology too.

Apart from the normal run of services, baptism and confirmation classes, other special occasions were honoured, such as milestones in a person's marriage, in thanksgiving for a specific event in the life of a parishioner. Then of course there were the inevitable funerals and cremations, as well as weddings, which were always a joy for all concerned. I always felt it a great honour to be part of such occasions, even if it sometimes meant being taken out of one's own comfort zone. To give but one example, a very devout parishioner was diagnosed with cancer. She asked me if I would take a healing service for her. Charles Lucas had also developed cancer and asked to be involved in the service. So I devised a form of service within the framework of the sacrament of communion. At a specific moment they both approached the altar and in the presence of their immediate families, I laid my hands on them, praying for healing. Charles Lucas sadly continued to decline and died shortly afterwards. But Eileen improved rapidly and was declared free from cancer. Twenty years on and she is still active in the parish and swears that it was the healing service that freed her from cancer.

OUTREACH IN THE PARISH

I said in my introduction to Warnham that my desire would be that the church would minister to every soul in the parish, and not only to those who worshipped within its walls. If the mountain would not come to Mohamed, then Mohamed had to come to the mountain! There were many ways to make this possible and most of them involved activities outside the church building. The most successful was to run a village fete. This had the double advantage of involving large numbers of villagers, as well as raising a good deal of money. Such fetes have been a part of my ministry in every place I have served, including Dar es Salaam, Bangkok, Thailand and Rotterdam. In every case, building on them year by year. They became an annual event and after initial reluctance by some to become involved, proved to be one of the highlights of the year. I go on to describe a typical fete in my last parish, Streat and Westmeston, later in the book, but suffice to say, they all followed the same pattern and became increasingly successful.

Another method of outreach was to organise outdoor services. The ideal place was on the village green or in a large garden of one of the houses in the village. As a centrepiece for the service, we had access to a 12-foot high cross, made up (rather like a jigsaw) of separate pieces of wood which when all put in place completed the cross with a biblical inscription on it. Again I will leave a description of the service to the last one I organised in Streat; like the fetes they achieved their purpose in extending the ministry of the church to all.

I have been asked whether there is much difference between being a padre in a mission and a priest in a parish. The answer is, 'Yes, there is!' A padre's ministry is aimed at a special group of people. With the Missions to Seamen, it is obviously seafarers, irrespective of nationality, colour or creed. A vicar in a parish, on the other hand, has the cure of souls of everyone in that parish. There is a great difference between the two. Baptisms and confirmations in the mission were usually of adults who hadn't been baptised when they were children. These candidates were inevitably very devoted and took their baptism or confirmation very seriously. It came as a great shock, therefore, with my first confirmation class in the parish, which consisted of about ten children aged about ten or eleven who had been waiting for me to arrive. They didn't take the classes seriously at all. In almost every case, they were there because of their parents' insistence. I felt uncomfortable with the classes. Some of the boys were more interested in the girls and the girls in responding with giggles. The contrast between this class and that held for seamen was painfully obvious. I agonised about what to do and finally decided that they were not ready yet for confirmation, so I called them all together and told them that I was not prepared to present them to the bishop at this time. The children didn't seem to be unduly worried, but their parents were and I had some very difficult meetings, but I stuck to my guns. I waited about three months before announcing that confirmation classes would shortly be resumed. At the first meeting I told them that I retained the right to remove from the class any whom I felt were not yet ready to be confirmed. About three quarters of the original class made up about half of the present candidates. The class, unlike the previously aborted one, went very well and it was with great joy that eventually I presented them all to the bishop for confirmation. All's well that ends well!

Then, occasionally, something out of the ordinary would crop up. Three instances spring to the mind. The first occurred as I was returning home from house visiting late one afternoon. I noticed an ambulance was parked in an unusual place. Not, as one would expect, outside a house but by a path on the edge of a field. Intrigued I followed the path for about 100 yards and came across an open ditch, I would guess was about 30-feet deep. I then remembered that workmen were laying a new sewer pipe into the village, hence the ditch. I followed the line of the trench and saw great activity about 100 yards away. As I neared the scene, I could see that the trench had collapsed and to my horror I quickly learnt that a workman was buried beneath the fall. Workmen were frantically trying to clear the fall, but not alas very successfully. Everyone took their turn in trying to reach the trapped man, but progress was painfully slow. Shortly after I arrived came a fire engine crew and also the emergency doctor. It took about two hours to final reach the victim and no one was surprised when the doctor pronounced him dead. With the aid of a stretcher he was finally lifted to the surface. In the meantime, I had been talking to the remaining workmen, offering what solace I could. I could see that the trench was just beyond the back garden of one of the houses in the village, whose occupants proved most helpful and provided cups of tea for all. They also gave permission for the body to be brought through their back garden. Once there, I asked his work mates whether they would like me to say some prayers. And the answer was a heartfelt yes. I was very impressed how the firemen and ambulance crew retreated from the immediate scene and so surrounded by his work mates, we held a simple service for Mr Forbes that proved to be very moving and deeply appreciated. The victim was a married man with young children, whom I understood received compensation from the firm.

The second saga was very different but equally moving. It concerned a mother and three children who recently moved into the village from South Africa. They immediately became faithful members of the congregation. The mother was extremely intelligent and the children delightful. I very quickly got to know them well. The youngest was christened and the eldest attended confirmation classes. All three children attended Farlington School, a private establishment, highly regarded and expensive. As there was no husband or apparent source of income, it did cross my mind how she was going to pay the fees. I subsequently learnt she told the head teacher that she was going to set up an ostrich farm in the village, which would prove very profitable and once established, she would clear all her debts. She let it be known that she had a large herd of ostriches that would shortly be arriving in the UK. She convinced the local council to let her have a temporary home on some local land which she would farm. She also persuaded various people to lend her money to get the project up and running. She had a very compelling manner, as I was soon to find out. Her approach to so many was that she would shortly be opening up an ostrich farm that would reap high financial rewards. The repayment for money lent would be doubled within a very short time. All of this turned out to be a con and I know that many villagers were taken in, as were others from Warnham and Horsham. Particularly upsetting was the case of a young man from Horsham who loaned her his life savings of about £2,500. He came to see me in great distress, asking if I could get his money back, which of course I couldn't. I was not surprised to read in the *Daily Mail* that some members of the royal family had also been conned into lending her money.

But even more distressing was her dealings with her children. She apparently had a form of Munchausen's syndrome, which manifested itself in many ways, but all with the same basic objective: to bring attention and sympathy to herself. To achieve this end she would lie about a situation or a person and make that situation worse by exaggerating even more. If continued undetected it could lead to very serious consequences, even to death itself. To give but one example, she told me that her youngest daughter had been badly mauled by a lion and she also volunteered the information that her husband was dead. By now the Social Services had become involved, partly because the headmistress of Farlington School had expressed concern about her behaviour with the children. Social Services also contacted me about their concerns and I was able to give examples of unnatural behaviour. She told her children that their father had died when in fact he was very much alive. He had been contacted by Social Services and was shortly coming to the UK to visit his children. Armed with this information, I confronted her in her house. She eventually admitted that she had lied to her children, but refused to tell them, so the lot fell on me. After they returned from school I met them in their house and as gently as possible, broke the news that their father was in fact still alive and was planning shortly to come and visit them. The youngest burst into tears, the second followed suit and the eldest went screaming out of the room and house. I found her later in the church. In the meantime, I did my best to comfort the other two. We had now moved into the age where one was not allowed to touch children, but I didn't hesitate to cuddle both of them and continued to do so until they regained some composure.

By now Social Services had decided to remove the children and to take them into care. They decided upon a date and asked me if I would be with the mother when they came to tell her. They were going to pick up the three children from school at the end of the day and take them to a foster home. Unfortunately she had kept the smallest child at home that day, so they had to take her from home. Needless to say, it was a very difficult and traumatic time. Both mother and child were extremely stressed. I did my best, which unfortunately, in the circumstances, wasn't very much.

Social Services gave me the foster house address and asked me to visit them. Actually I did far more because, until other arrangements could be made, I picked the children up in the morning, took them to school and collected them at the end of the day. Everyone in the village knew that the children had been taken from their mother, but didn't know why. They also knew that I was involved but I couldn't enlighten them as to why. The village was divided right down the middle and for those who opposed, I became the whipping block.

Once a week I took them to a safe house in Horsham, where they met their mother. A member of Social Services was present throughout that time. Actually the children coped very well given the circumstances, including meeting their father when he arrived from South Africa. I believe that the mother was also given counselling and as far as I can remember, after about six months, the children were returned to her care. As quickly as she arrived in Warnham, she departed and we saw them no more. We learnt from the press about a month after their departure that she had conned money from a member of the Royal Family, so the saga continued. The village gradually returned to normal and the press cuttings helped to put the case to bed.

One would think that in a little village like Warnham nothing extraordinary would happen, so you can imagine the reaction when one of its young men was charged with murder! He was courting a young lady from Horsham, without the approval of her father, who became incensed when he learnt that she was pregnant. Tempers flared and blows were struck. Sadly the father died from his wounds. The man was arrested and charged with murder. He was detained in Lewes prison, where I visited him. Then two things happened; his girlfriend produced a lovely bouncing boy and his own father died. The prison authorities gave him permission to attend his father's funeral. He arrived at his house, handcuffed to two of the warders, but was then allowed upstairs, where his girlfriend and baby were waiting to greet him. About half an hour later, they called him down and then we all went off to the funeral. Very few people realised that he was in handcuffs and the service continued without any problems. Until his death, the father ran a mobile snack bar on a layby about two miles from the village. Although his mother had to cope with a son in prison and the death of her husband, she insisted on keeping the business going. So instead of counselling in a lounge in a house, I found myself sitting in a layby, usually with a cooked sausage on a plate and a cup of tea in a scalding mug in my hands. I am not sure why, but the son received a surprisingly short sentence and life continued after his release. As for me, it added yet another dimension of counselling to my already considerable portfolio and proved me wrong when I said at the beginning of my incumbency that I wouldn't experience anything new.

HEALTH PROBLEMS

Before I realised it, I had been in Warnham for five years, which by coincidence came at a time when I became quite ill. The doctor was not sure what the problem was, eventually coming to the conclusion that I had picked up a virus. Whatever it was, it left me weak, aching in every joint and it really pulled me down. In the end, he signed me off work and I went up to stay with my daughter, Elizabeth. Loving care had the desired effect and after about four weeks, the virus left as quickly as it had arrived and I was able to return to work. I have been known to say that sometimes in illness the Good Lord makes you lie down so you can look up! During this forced break I reflected on where I was and if it was where I wanted to be. Although there was plenty more to be achieved in the parish, I felt it was now on the right path and possibly another could take it further forward. I felt an increasing desire to write my autobiography, which time and time again seemed to end up on the back burner. I have always tried to put people before things and the time that I intended to devote to my book often became taken up with the needs of others.

The one exception was on the golf course. I had started playing with two parishioner friends, once a week, but as any golfer will tell you one has to play more than once a week if you hope to improve. When I went to Dar es Salaam I was given a set of golf clubs, but was always too busy to use them. In fact I lent them out to visiting seamen. I also felt I would like to become more involved with my growing family and determined to raise the matter with Charles Lucas, patron and church warden, once safely back in the parish. Charles was horrified at the suggestion and assured me that there was plenty more still to achieve at Warnham. 'So please carry on,' he said, and I did.

A VISIT TO CHINA

Another parishioner with whom I became very friendly was Dennis Hill. He didn't actually live in Warnham, but in the next village. Shortly after I first knew him, his wife sadly died. He became a regular communicant and such was his attendance that he almost became a problem! He loved the 8.00 a.m. Holy Communion and apart from sickness, never failed to be there in his usual place. But he also loved music and singing, which meant that he was at the 10.00 a.m. communion as well. Yes, you've guessed it, he liked evensong too. He used to say to me, 'I don't mind hearing the same sermon twice,' but his presence at all three services on a Sunday meant that I needed at least two sermons every Sunday and even, on some occasions, three! But it's an ill wind that doesn't bring some relief, because, through his friendship, two important events enriched my life.

The first arose when he told me he wanted to visit China and would I go with him? During my time in Hong Kong I had often been up to the Chinese border, but had never crossed it. During the course of my ship visiting, I had visited many Chinese ships, but never got past the concierge stationed at the top of the gangway. Since then I had always yearned to overcome that barrier, so it took very little persuasion to agree. It proved to be a fascinating fortnight, including visiting the Forbidden City and climbing the Great Wall of China. Whether one liked it or not, some of the arranged outings were political in nature but nonetheless impressive. There was a very full programme of events. One I particularly remember was a visit to a giant sports stadium devoted entirely to table tennis, at least twelve tables in a row, all occupied by young aspiring players. Dennis knew that I used to play to quite a high standard and volunteered this information to our Chinese guide. Before I could say Jack Robinson, there I was, bat in hand, at the opposite end of the table facing a young Chinese player. All other activity in the hall stopped and before the first ball was served, there was I at the centre of an international! He proved to be too good for me and every winning shot was greeted by cheers from everyone, except our little party, who had little or nothing to cheer about.

We had been advised not to give money but presents, such as pens and pencils, at the end of the match, so I presented the winner with a rather nice pen and pencil set, which was received with a huge smile of pleasure from my opponent and rapturous applause by the other players.

On another occasion I was not as happy. I have always been a very keen philatelist and had over the years built up a very substantial collection of stamps, including those from China. When visiting the Forbidden City there were the inevitable touts selling their wares. Like many countries, China produced a yearly stamp collection in a folder. There were many touts selling them; I bargained and purchased one such folder of the current year, but within seconds I was surrounded with others with previous years' folders, all trying to pass them to me. But just then our coach driver blew his horn and I could see that I was the only passenger not on board, so I left them and made my way to the awaiting coach. Not to be outdone, they followed me and as I drew ever nearer to the coach, so the price of the folders fell alarmingly. Finally, at a price I just couldn't reject, I quickly selected eight folders and paying a ridiculous price, jumped on the bus and away. They, however, had the last laugh. The folders were all full, but with odd stamps from various countries that were of no use to me at all!

The tour provided activities for every day, including the Sunday. We had heard of the growth of the Chinese Church and very much wanted to experience being a part of it, so whilst the rest of the group went to visit a local port, Dennis and I determined to find and worship with a Chinese congregation. The hotel arranged for a taxi to take us to one of the churches. We sped to a part of Beijing that was not familiar to us and went through more and more back streets, getting narrower and narrower. Eventually the taxi stopped and the driver signalled for us to get out. He indicated he could go no further, but called a rickshaw, telling him where we wanted to go. After what seemed an age, we stopped outside a building, which we then saw resembled in some ways a church. Only it had obviously been enlarged at least three times. We entered to find a congregation of around 500 souls listening intently to a sermon. We were met on arrival by an usher who led us to a part of the church which was obviously reserved for foreigners. Apart from the fact that the seats were better than others around us, there were also earphones which were translating the service into English. True, we had to try about four different earphones before we found two that worked, but thereafter all was fine. It was a lady preacher (whose sermon lasted about three-quarters of an hour) but no one seemed to mind. The singing of the hymns was inspirational and their memory remained with me for the rest of the day, indeed through the night as well.

Our hotel was in the centre of Beijing and from the twelfth floor I was able to look out towards Tiananmen Square. I suddenly felt compelled to stand tall in the window, with arms outstretched and give a blessing. That's exactly what I did. My arms did not depict the cross, but a tank advancing across the square with a student standing defiantly in front of it. That moment became for me the highlight of the tour.

After a remarkable event, it is often said, 'Beat that!' Well, in my case, I was able to. Dennis was a very high-ranking Freemason and invited me to preach at a special service designed for other Masons at Hurstpierpoint College Chapel. The Bible is used constantly in Masonic circles, so I felt very happy to preach on it. After the service was over, tea was laid on in the refectory. I took this opportunity to meet people and in due course came to Dennis and his three lady guests who were seated on a settee. I had some general conversation with them and then moved on. A little later I met Dennis who was getting tea for his guests.

'What do you think of my harem?' he jokingly asked me. To be honest at that time I could hardly remember what any of them looked like, but in keeping with his question, I said I liked the lady on the right and then thought no more of it. Driving his guests home after the service, Dennis told them that I fancied the lady on the right. A discussion then ensued. 'What did I mean by the lady on the right?' If I meant looking down at them then the right was on the right. But if I meant from the ladies sitting on the settee, then it would mean the lady on the left. Be that as it may, the two at either end of the settee decided to cook a meal for me at Dennis's house. The lady in the middle disappeared without trace! On the due day, I arrived at his house to be greeted by Dennis; we then sat down to await the ladies' arrival. The first lady to appear came with a dog. She then complained that Dennis had no grass on his back garden for her dog to play on. She then, in no uncertain terms, told us that after the lunch we all had to take the dog for a walk. Even before the second lady had arrived I had made up my mind as to whom I meant when I said the lady on the right. The second lady duly arrived with a smile on her face, which confirmed my decision.

I must say that, between them, they provided an excellent meal, the preparation of which they shared. After lunch was completed, sure enough, we were told it was time to take the dog for a walk. Dennis declined and I said I should remain to look after my friend. The lady with a smile I learnt was a widow called Millie and as far as I was concerned, she had won hands down. But that was not the end of the story. We continued to see each other and despite Dennis's misgivings (Bexhill, where she lived, was a long way from Warnham), our friendship blossomed and ended in marriage shortly after I retired from Warnham. To find love in one's seventies is a blessing indeed, a blessing that has continued to this day. Not only did I find myself a loving wife,

Our wedding day, 12 June 1990.

I was quickly accepted by all of Millie's family, which includes four great grandchildren. Being married to a clergyman can be a real challenge, especially if started later in life, but Millie has coped admirably. I am a very lucky man.

My writings show very clearly that a priest never knows what dramas will unfold during the course of his ministry. This is not surprising perhaps during my time in Tanzania, Thailand and Rotterdam, but not equally so in what one would assume to be a sleepy village like Warnham. But dramas there were the sudden arrival on one's doorstep of tramps or others perhaps just out of prison. A favourite line was that they wanted the fare to get them back home. One even tried to sell me one of his paintings. Hard luck stories of every imaginable kind would pour forth from their lips, but in a very short time the mood could change dramatically, especially if their request was turned down. Things got so bad that the diocese issued guidelines on how to deal with such a situation. One suggestion was that every vicarage should have a chain on their front door. I always tried at first to be as sympathetic as possible, except when their story was obviously a load of rubbish. In such cases I used to get very annoyed, taking it as an insult to my intelligence.

Some cases, however, were genuine and in such cases I did try and help. As stated before, Burmese refugees would often say, 'If you can only get to Canon John's church in Bangkok you will be all right.' Imagine my surprise, therefore, that on more than one occasion, who would appear on my doorstep in Warnham? A Burmese who had made his way illegally to the UK, using a similar slogan, 'If you can get to Canon John in Warnham you will be all right!'

The market town of Horsham was about 3 miles from Warnham and I suppose, inevitably, some calls for help would come from there. Reputations (whether good or bad) spread beyond normal boundaries, so I occasionally received cries for help from other sources. I sometimes couldn't help wondering whether I was considered a soft touch! I was comforted by the example of the Pope John XXIII when he was a cardinal. He was known to say when confronted by queues of people, 'If only one person in ten was genuine in their need, then no matter if I was taken for a ride by the other nine!'

One cry for help had nothing to do with money. The phone rang and on the other end was a youngish-sounding lady, obviously in a very distressed state. After asking my name, she said someone had told her that I could help. It transpired that she had been using Tarot

Christmas is coming!

cards and crystals in her house, and holding meetings with such likeminded folks. Then strange and unexpected events started happening and she believed her house had been taken over by the devil. Her small children were badly affected and her husband, who didn't approve of what she had been doing, was threatening to break up the marriage. One fact was that the house became unnaturally cold. Could I please come immediately to try and put things right? I must admit that when I entered it did indeed seem unnaturally cold. Today there are specially prepared priests in every diocese who are trained in dealing with such matters, but not at this time, so I had to try and deal with it myself.

Two things had to happen. The first was to cleanse the family from the power of sin and this required confession, before absolution. They were a non-churchgoing family, so the concept of confessing sins to a priest was hard to accept. I insisted, however, and after instruction on how to make a confession, confessions did take place. The next step was to visit every room in the house, exorcising as we went. I don't know about the family but I found the whole exercise very trying and felt exhausted after it was over. I don't know what the experts thought about it all, but I do know that it had the desired effect both with the couple and the house. I kept in touch for a while, but then considered the job done and referred them to their local church. Although they may not have realised it themselves, such people are seeking a form of spirituality, not necessary religious, but spiritual nevertheless. There is a great need for this whole area to be examined and I do hope that the right sort of person does indeed take up the challenge.

During my time at Warnham I came to see that in running a parish there was a similarity with being at sea, which had occupied so much of my ministry. Most of the time the sea is calm and one travels on untroubled waters. But at times the sea becomes violent, as the moving book *The Cruel Sea* so aptly describes it. Most of my time in Warnham was clear sailing, allowing the church to honour its cycle of services and other church activities, to provide its parishioners with a regular pattern of worship and fellowship, and to constantly enable St Margaret's to be engaged in building up the body of Christ. Sure there were storms but most of them were in a teacup, and soon put to rights. Rather like, if you think about it, most of our lives, there is little to write home about, although it is all an essential part of our pilgrimages through life. So it is that I can cover my time at Warnham in less than forty pages. All good things they say come to an end and that's what happened to me. I hadn't realised it but no priest can have the cure of souls of a parish after reaching seventy years of age. So it

Bishops Lindsay and Down at my farewell service.

The farewell party.

was that amongst my mail one day was a letter from the diocese informing me that as I was approaching seventy, I would have to resign my living. Bishop Lindsay softened the blow by telling me that he would issue me with a licence to continue in my ministry after retirement, which he did.

The parish gave me a wonderful farewell service, attended not only by the local residents, but by friends from far afield. There were actually past parishioners from Tanzania, Thailand and the Netherlands present at the service, followed by a lavish reception in the village hall, when I was presented with some wonderful presents, including a cheque for well over £3,000. The end amount was actually considerably higher than this as late gifts rolled in. I raised a laugh when I told the guests that this was one cheque that was not going into the church's coffers!

Streat and Westmeston (2000–2011)

At this time I moved to a flat in Horsham in the parish of Roffey where I became active in priesthood under a wonderful priest, Kevin Agnew. He had a lovely family who also made me so welcome. It was shortly after moving to Horsham that Millie and I settled down in our new flat, which we were convinced would be our last move. But this was not to be. Within months of my retirement, Bishop Lindsay told me of two parishes that were without a priest and, as he put it, they were dying for a young and energetic priest to look after them! He suggested that I went and had a look around both parishes to see if I thought either of them were suitable. If accepted I would be appointed as priest in charge, on half salary. This meant that I would be there under the bishop's pleasure, unlike being an incumbent, where one cannot be moved unless there are serious reasons for doing so.

Streat parish church.

The accommodation was a bungalow, which Millie liked very much. As I thought that Streat and Westmeston would be the right choice, I met with the wardens of both churches, who apparently approved of my appointment, and so it came to pass that I was duly installed as priest in charge.

The Lord works in a mysterious way, his wonders to perform. Prior to moving to Streat and Westmeston, I had served in major cities across the world – in the docklands of London; in Victoria, Hong Kong; in Dar es Salaam, Tanzania; in Bangkok, Thailand; in Rotterdam, Holland – and now, finally not in a city or town, or even a village, but in a hamlet called Streat of less than a hundred houses with no shop, pub or post office. Likewise, Westmeston was a village with only a church. Streat Church had never even adopted a patron saint. To some it might appear as if my ministry was on a downward slope! Could I see in it a similar pattern I asked myself?

After ordination I was curate for only two years (five was not uncommon during the eighties) then chaplain with the Missions to Seamen. Shortly afterwards I was appointed Archdeacon of Dar es Salaam and then vicar general, holding the fort for the bishop when he was out of his diocese. When I finally left the diocese after twelve years, I was made a canon emeritus. Shortly afterwards I was honoured with the OBE (Other Brethren's Efforts!). This meant I had a title both before and after my name. But thereafter was it downhill all the way? To reiterate what I am sure I have said before, promotion in the church is being where God wants you to be! What particularly, I wondered, did God want of me here? I was soon to find out.

Bishop Lindsay told me that I would be the last priest appointed to Streat and Westmeston. After my departure the two parishes would be united with Ditchling. When I informed the wardens of this, there was little or no reaction. They had heard all that before, they told me, concerning the appointment of the last three priests. I, nevertheless, accepted the bishop's version and planned accordingly. I was determined that it wouldn't be a takeover bid (Ditchling being the largest of the three), but equals coming together. Secondly I was determined that Streat and Westmeston would be united, acting as one during and after the merger. This, alas, was not entirely the present situation. There were strong characters in both hamlets, each prepared to fight for their own corner. In fact rivalry had existed between the two hamlets way back into history, as a brief resume will show.

THE HISTORY

Streat and Westmeston had remained separate civil parishes, but, from time to time, the unsought unification of the churches *has* caused problems. Rumour has it that conflict has existed since the Battle of Lewes in 1264, one hamlet supporting King Henry III and the other the English barons. More likely, conflict occurred when there was an issue affecting only one church which was seen to be considered jointly. With one priest serving two parishes and located in the smaller parish, some tension was occasionally inevitable. In theory there was not a single PCC but rather two PCCs choosing to work as one; issues affecting one church alone could be decided by PCC members from that parish, but when cash was involved it had to be a joint decision.

In recent times, Streat was accused of trying to dictate to Westmeston concerning the removal of pews in their church. If there was to be any conflict at the merger then I was determined that Streat and Westmeston would be united in purpose. This apart, the financial state of the three would be paramount. I therefore saw my priorities as being to put the parish on a strong financial base, with both churches in a good state of repair; to unite Streat and Westmeston in their desire to forward the Kingdom of God; to produce a mission statement to show the way, the truth and the life. A special away day was planned for the PCC to compose a Mission Statement.

THE MISSION STATEMENT

We welcome all to join us in the worship of God and of his Son, Jesus Christ, Our Lord. We aim...
    To be a loving community through sharing Christ's Gospel
    To be a learning community growing in faith
    To be a worshipping community guided by the Holy Spirit
    To be a witnessing community
    To encourage all into the fellowship of the Church
    To be prayerfully and financially supportive of the worldwide mission of the Church

To achieve this aim would only be possible through the grace of Almighty God and the support of the congregation. The reason I wrote my biography In the first place was to try and show the Holy Spirit at work in an ordinary priest's ministry. I just pray that it does.

They say that small is beautiful. On the other hand, in such a situation you can often find large stones in small ponds and sadly this was the situation when I arrived – some good souls doing more than one job. One such person was John Eastwood, secretary and member of the PCC, editor of the parish magazine, church warden of Westmeston (although he actually lived in Streat!). Furthermore, he was overseeing all the children's work and taking all the family services. If all of this were not enough, it was well known that he was a personal friend of the archdeacon! He could well be forgiven if all this proved too much for him, which sadly proved to be the case. The wardens confided in me that things had got completely out of hand.

For a start, concerning the minutes of the PCC, they appeared in a form that reflected the secretary's understanding of the meetings rather than what actually occurred. If there was a topic with which he strongly disagreed he included in the minutes his own views at great length on the subject. But worse was to follow. If a decision was made with which he disagreed, it was left out completely. Under his editorship, no mention was made of the various rotas that prove to be the lifeblood of any successful church system. The PCC agreed that in future all rotas would be displayed in the magazine. Alas, like Mother Hubbard's cupboard, the magazine was bare!

Hence followed my first clash. I called on him in his large and impressive home and eying him eyeball to eyeball, told him that the parish rotas had to be included in the magazine. Did they? No. As a compromise he printed them out on separate sheets. I determined there and then that I would relieve him of being secretary of the PCC and also editor of the parish magazine. What happened next only confirmed my decision, but first I should explain that under the present timing of services it was impossible for the vicar to be present at them all. It meant he wouldn't be able to attend the monthly family service. This wasn't a problem, however, because all such services were taken by – yes, you've guessed it – our multi-talented friend John. He could write letters too. To my amazement, I received a letter from him which began, 'I do hope that you will be able to attend the family service at least once or twice in the year! Children's work has always been an essential part of my ministry and I intend it to remain so.'

So came my second eyeball to eyeball meeting, when I told him that I was going to change the time of services so that I could be present at every service. I told him that I valued his contribution and wanted him to continue, but that I needed to be heavily involved too. Then came the bombshell. He said that the archdeacon had told him he could continue to take the children's services, even after the new priest was appointed! I pointed out that if the archdeacon did say that then he was completely out of order. He had no authority to make such a decision. And I knew this because I had been an archdeacon myself.

Understandably, relationships between us became more and more strained, especially when he was relieved of service in various areas. I was most fortunate that Sir Mark Moody Stuart agreed to be Church Warden of Westmeston, so making a perfect team with Doreen Kallman, the other church warden. He was duly elected and fitted in perfectly; his wisdom and knowledge brought great benefits to the parish. We were also very blessed when Margaret Bovill took over as secretary. The changes sadly led to John's non-church attendance. His was the only family (that I am aware of) throughout my ministry that I lost. This led to heartache on my part, but, on reflection, it seemed inevitable.

The times of the services were changed, so I was able to attend every single one. I've always said that if the Good Lord doesn't give, He sends; well, he gave me the most wonderful team of helpers, so that the children's services actually went from strength to strength. So much so that visitors from other parishes came to see how we conducted them (and ourselves). I remember, on one occasion, the theme was the house built upon the sand rather than rock. We had a good amount of sand spread on the floor of the church, complete with buckets and spades, so that the children were actually able to build sandcastles; this they did with great glee. Then I came along and with a large bucket of water, destroyed them all in one fell swoop! The visitors' eyes were a sight to behold, but the children certainly got the message. As we rectified the mess after the service was over, which took a considerable amount of time and effort, all agreed that it was well worth while.

A sign of a good team, incidentally, is not only are they are prepared to get everything ready, but also to help clear up afterwards! In this the team excelled.

Before I move on, I must refer to John Eastwood once more. The reader might think that he was not a very nice person but the opposite was true. The fact that he accepted so many chores shows a willing heart, generous in the giving of time and talents. Being church warden of Westmeston, for example, came about because there was no one else who would take it on. As I have already said, the fact that he ceased to be a member of the congregation caused me much pain, but another congregation (from a local chapel) benefited, so all was not lost.

Talking of accolades, it is always dangerous to mention people by name, for fear that one forgets to mention someone who should have been there in large bold print. But I must give mention to Derek Walker and Colin Juniper, being the church wardens for Streat, and their wives, Lynette and Jane. They never once refused an appeal for help or support.

A special word about Westmeston, which heavily relied on Church Warden Doreen Kallman, ably supported by husband, Gerald, and son, Paul, for its very existence. Nothing connected with the church was too much bother. Doreen was utterly reliable and efficient to boot. Being a one-man band can have its problems, but her dedication and determination overcame them all. We were all delighted when, in recognition of her work, she was invited to a party at Buckingham Palace.

Then there were the ordinary members of the congregation: too many to mention by name, but all vital members of the body of Christ, all totally committed to the mission of the church. One such person was Myrtle Skelton, a past church warden and long-time member of the PCC. I have mentioned before that things were not always harmonious between the two hamlets. I was told of one PCC meeting when matters became so heated that it almost came to blows. Then Myrtle spoke out. She berated those at the heart of the argument and said, 'We must stop talking like heathens and instead pray like Christians.' So she did and as she did, peace descended upon the gathering and the chastened members resumed the meeting without any of the tension that existed before. Apart from the many tasks she undertook in the parish, she became heavily involved in helping the homeless in Brighton. She was given a presentation from the Mayor of Brighton when she retired.

I must also mention the many residents of Streat and Westmeston who were not regular members of the congregation, but who came up trumps when appealed to, whether in cash or kind!

They say that the proof of the pudding is in the eating. Ours was delicious. I can give no better example than by describing a fete we held in August 2005, in the hall and grounds of Westmeston Parish

a
Weekend to Remember'

August 2005

we love music

Heathfield Brass Band

What a dazzling Fete!! It was blazing hot so much so that a camel came wandering in thinking he had found an oasis! The stars came with beaming smiles, happy to sign autographs and enjoy the day. The food was delicious - gorgeous hog roast and hot dogs and scrumptious afternoon teas with exquisite home made dreamy cakes. The stalls were busy all day long with good natured children and parents happily enjoying themselves and eating ice creams all serenaded with music, pipes, Victorian drama, dancing and bells echoing. What a stunning Fete!
                                                                          Margaret Bovill

Ditchling choir

A bus load from an old people's home was delayed in the traffic, so just dropped in. One old lady, with a zimmer frame, was seen to be ordering three pints of Harvey Best Bitter. Her friend chipped in *'You won't walk to the top of the South Downs with that inside you!'*

Vera Lynn judges the fancy dress

hot dogs

Olivia (6) "*I really liked the playing the cards game and I rang the bells.*"

Lucy (9) "*I was very excited when I got to hold hands with Vera Lynn, especially because we are singing her songs at school*

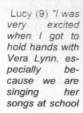

cakes

22

'Weekend to Remember'

Streat & Westmeston CHURCH FETE

the hog roast

Lucy Benjamin opens the fete.

'Weekend to Remember'

I woke up at 3 50 am on the morning of the fete, from my sleep on the concrete ramp at the back of the village hall to hear Alan Taylor saying *"are you awake Lance, its time to get the pig on?"* It was still dark but we watched the sky lighten and the arrival of the most beautiful day. *Lance Smith*

tea

One of the ladies serving the cream teas was asked *'Please can you let me have the name of the professional Catering Company that you used'*.

Will the owner of the bull terrier that ran amok among the Pipe band dancers please come forward for a special prize! Congratulations to the pipers for carrying on as if nothing had happened.

Katie (12) *"The entertainment was endless. The stalls were great fun. I really enjoyed watching the dancers and ringing the bells."*

1

'Weekend to Remember'

a

The weekend of the 16th & 17th July Fete and Open Air Service was the best weekend that I can remember in living memory of 60 yrs +. The wonderful clear blue skies, with just on a thousand people looking so happy as they walked and talked from stall to stall, or just sat quietly and watched the entertainment through the afternoon. Then came the uplifting open air service held on Sunday followed by a picnic.   *Doreen Kallman.*

Great community affair – at the Silent Auction many winners and losers commented on the warmth and spirit and music of the occasion: A huge effort soliciting prizes by Canon John and all who made such a wonderful variety possible. Donations from "signed Gift Aid declarations" will add an imminent £625 from the Inland Revenue – thank you, too, Mr Gordon Brown for your silent contribution to our Churches.
          Judy Moody-Stuart

This is a small selection of the 150+ photos submitted to the SWCM.

23

Hall. I can say with hand on heart that there wasn't a single family in the two hamlets who didn't help in one way or another.

It's possibly worth mentioning that during my time in the parish I visited every single house and family at least twice. Some say that house visiting is no longer a good use of time and effort. But, as far as I was concerned, this couldn't be further from the truth. Some of the residents, who never came to services at either of the two churches, would ask how the church was doing and when they could help organise the next event! 'If I can do anything then just let me know.'

They say that a good picture is worth a thousand words. I enclose therefore photos that tell their own story! Not only did the fete result in wonderful comradeship and harmony, it brought together folks from all parts of the parish, so healing many old wounds and creating a new atmosphere that was a joy to experience. The icing on the cake

6/8/05

Dear Father,

Whilst I address this to you officially, it is intended for all parishioners and congregation involved in the Streat and Westmeston Summer Fayre,

I was fortunate enough, over 30 years ago, to spend a short part of my childhood in the lovely village of Hassocks. As an adult I returned here, from Brighton, a few years ago with my husband. Our desire was to bring up our family in a smaller, more pleasant community than the one which my home town of Brighton had grown into.

As a result of living here, we enjoy the more simple things in life now; the local village market for example.

The fayre in your village was another example and the purpose of this letter is to thank you all for organising such a lovely family day.

The traditional games took me back to my childhood, rolling the tennis balls into the holes, coconut shys-I didn't even know how to play shove ha'penny I had to be shown! The gents who must have spent hours making their home made wine were also a treasure, I commented on how they must feel about us turning up our noses as we tried their "toiled over" home brews, but they were not phased.

And what a bargain all for just 50p!

As a sharp-nosed businesswoman I reckon you could increase the process of some of the stalls and still people would be happy to pay!

Thank you to the lovely lady who had bunched and tied lavender in ribbons-she was delighted that we bought 6 bunches and her home made mint jelly was superb!

In the world we live in now, where evil acts and not "loving thy neighbour"! appear to be commonplace, I commented to my husband how lovely it was to step back in time, to such innocent times and for me, that's what your village fayre allowed me to do. I am only young too, so for the older visitors it must have been even more of a treat. I felt like I had landed in Midsomer Village!

If I had not moved from Brighton I know I would ever have shared in the day(I wouldn't have known about it) and I couldn't help but say to my husband how those just a few minutes drive away in the city by the sea, didn't know what they were missing!

I have told all my family about the lovely time we had and we will be returning en masse!

Thank you all and very good luck for organising the next one..we cant wait!!

Kind Regards

Julia Mike and Grace Ridley

A fayre appreciation.

was the amount of money raised. When all the monies were counted up, it produced a profit of £11,000. Any reader who has been involved with such ventures will know that £2,000 or so for a fete was considered a wonderful result. £11,000 was almost unbelievable and helped to make the parish financially viable.

Incidentally, the reader may be wondering by now why Streat is spelt with an 'a' rather than an 'e'. The word derives from 'Strata', Latin for street. The spelling was changed in 1837 by the vicar, perhaps to avoid confusion with Street in Somerset, or to mark Queen Victoria's accession.

MY PROSTATE CANCER

It was around this time that biopsy tests revealed that I had the most aggressive form of prostate cancer. This necessitated the maximum amount of radioactivity treatment, some thirty-six sessions altogether, at Brighton General Hospital, between 10th February to 1st April 2005. No sooner had the dates been set than the parishioners compiled a list of drivers to take me, wait for the duration of the treatment and then bring me back home again. They were as good as their word, which not only meant that Millie was relieved of that responsibility, but also gave me an opportunity to get to know the volunteers very well, or even better, during the time spent together. Parking is normally a nightmare at the hospital, but luckily there was a special car park for cancer patients.

There was a lovely lady always present at the clinic. I suspect she was a volunteer whose duty seemed to be limited to keeping the area tidy. Because of the rota system, I often had different ladies escorting me five days running. I used to introduce them to all and sundry as my wife! One usually met the same people at the clinic, who soon caught on to what I was up to, but the poor kind lady to which I have already referred became utterly confused. She waited with bated breath to see what the morrow would bring. As luck would have it, I had a special treat to offer.

A few years earlier, I had the great joy of baptising triplets in Westmeston Church. They were Lucy, Edward and William Robinson. The font, incidentally, is the only working chalk font in the country. The whole family were very much involved in church activities. This meant that I knew the children very well and watched them grow. Not

The baptism of the Robinsons' triplets.

surprisingly, their parents were on the rota to take me for my cancer treatment. When the children knew what was to happen, they begged to be able to take Canon John to hospital too. Sure enough, the Land Rover, complete with the triplets, arrived promptly at my door to take me to hospital. I intended to introduce them as my children! Alas, when we arrived, they were all asleep, so I was unable to do so.

On the first two visits, there was little or no conversation among the patients, but I was able to break that mould and the atmosphere changed completely. I must say that the staff were wonderfully kind, so it almost became a pleasure to go for the treatment. Indeed, once the treatment was finished, it was as if a gap had been left unfilled. Nine years on, although I still have to go for three monthly injections, the cancer seems to be under complete control, for which I thank God and all those who work in the National Health Service. I wince when I hear criticisms of the NHS; I think of countries where I have worked where there is little or nothing like it and what there is is thanks only to Christian Charities.

HAROLD ROWLING

A name I haven't mentioned yet is Harold Rowling. This is an omission I must rectify now, because, without doubt, he is one of the best known characters in Westmeston and was the engine that powered most of the projects attempted and achieved. I was going to add 'by hook or by crook', which isn't strictly true, although he would go to great lengths to achieve his aim. He was one of the leading lights in making possible the Westmeston Parish Hall, which has proved to be a huge success, partly because Doreen Kallman has had the running of it since it came into operation. But to return to Harold, he was on most of the small committees, such as preserving footpaths for public use. He also was involved in the creation of a car park on the edge of the Downs, looking down to Westmeston and beyond.

Shortly before I took office, a strong difference of opinion arose amongst the congregation as to whether or not the pews should be replaced by chairs, the object being to give more flexibility. Harold strongly disagreed and petitioned names from local people, whether they were churchgoers or not, opposing the scheme. Consequently, the pews were not replaced. By the time of my arrival, Harold was getting on in years, although he still printed a local magazine, which was often considered controversial, and made his presence felt in many other ways. He still read the Bible in church, but would only use the King James version. He strongly disliked the version that was commonly used and said he wouldn't read his lesson from it. This was problematic, so I appealed to him to read from the same version as everyone else, so that everyone could follow the lesson that was being read. In protest he stopped reading lessons and only rarely came to church. I eventually heard from him again when he enquired whether or not he could be buried in his garden. I gave him the answer (yes, upon certain conditions), but pointed out that not every purchaser would appreciate having his remains in their garden! He also asked if he could be buried in the church graveyard. This was not possible as it had been closed long ago, once full. The church opened up a second graveyard, which was in current use. Thankfully he was still alive when I left the parish, so the problem didn't arise!

There is another person who deserves mention, but can't be named because he insisted his generosity be anonymous. It concerns my hearing aids. I have suffered with partial deafness (inherited from my mother) since my late teens. Over the years my hearing has deteriorated;

consequently, I have needed hearing aids ever since. My first aid was not very good (although quite expensive) and after about five years, it had lost its efficiency to the extent that I had to push the hearing mechanism to its limit. The trouble (as any user will testify) was that a strong whistling ensued. I was aware that my ministry was being affected. For example, a person making their confession or suffering illness inevitably speaks quietly. One cannot delve deeply into the confession and can only ask a question to clarify the situation. On one occasion I was hearing the confession of a lady who confessed to adultery. Because she was speaking quietly I didn't hear the extent of her infidelity. Apparently I asked how many times in such a way that it appeared I was appalled at the number – '*How* many times?!'

This episode convinced me that I needed to do something about my hearing or else terminate my ministry, but funds were tight. However, one day, the generous parishioner asked Millie if I would be offended if he purchased the newest and latest aids for me. The kind offer then came as a Godsend, which I accepted. As a consequence, eight years on and I am still active, despite retiring three times! And I am now into my eighty-sixth year.

THE WELCOME BOOKLET

Wherever I have served I have found that newcomers to the area or parish can find it difficult to settle down and find their feet. Consequently it has been my practice to issue a welcome booklet, obviously containing useful information, a brief history, and names of officers and helpful people. The welcome booklet for Streat and Westmeston proved so helpful that we gave one to all the residents in the parish.

CHRISTIAN STEWARDSHIP

I have already mentioned that the two essential ingredients of Christian Stewardship are time and talents. Church Wardens are, in theory, only appointed for a certain length of time, although in smaller parishes it is not always possible to find a replacement. In Streat we were blessed in having potential candidates, so when the time came for Colin Juniper to retire, I felt drawn to one Michael Sewell as his successor. Apart from being a committed Christian, he had many talents, including do-it-yourself expertise. He had supported me in all ventures; indeed, without his input the results achieved would not have been possible. A man with such energy of necessity had many hobbies, including sailing. This would mean that he couldn't be in church every Sunday, so when I approached him he hesitated in taking on this extra office. I assured him that this would be no obstacle, especially because his wife, Sue (behind every good man there is a woman!), would normally be present when he was away. So Mike became the church Warden of Streat and I can honestly say, not once during my ministry did I ever find him wanting. Sue, although not always enjoying the best of health, likewise became a pillar of strength. So I became blessed with the perfect team.

MUSIC IN THE PARISH

Whilst acknowledging that the strength of a parish lies in its congregation, there are other factors that enhance the worship, none more so than music. Imagine then my disappointment when I discovered that there were no choirs in the parish. Streat was extremely fortunate in having as its organist Lynette Walker, but Westmeston had to rely on tapes containing hymns, except for the monthly children's service, when Lyn Bond obliged. Lyn also played for one of the churches in a nearby parish, but I was overjoyed when she agreed to play for all services at Westmeston. Lynette and Lyn also covered for each other when necessary, so not once in all my time in the parish were we without an organist for a service. This also applied to weddings and funerals, and both organists declined to receive a fee for the normal church services. This is the only parish in which I have served where this has occurred. Despite the generosity and dedication shown by them both, there were times, especially at special services, when a choir would have been a great asset. But I knew, because of the size of the parish, that it would not be possible to raise one choir, let alone two, to sing at every service, so I hit upon the idea of forming one choir just to sing at special services, as well as at social events in the parish. So was born the Jubilee Choir.

My thinking came at a time when we were making preparations to honour the Queen's Golden Jubilee in June 2002, and I could see just how much the celebration would be enhanced if we had a choir. I knew that Jinks McGrath sang in a choir elsewhere, so she was the obvious person to share my hope. She responded wonderfully. Lynette also agreed to play for them. About twelve good folks turned up for the first gathering and the first time I heard them singing, the hairs stood up on the back of my head. In a very short time others joined rehearsals and the choir was ready. They sang for the first time at the Queen's Jubilee service at St Martin's church. I know that many listened, spellbound to the anthems. I also noted that with a choir leading the singing, the congregation responded in kind. So the Jubilee Choir came into being and still flourishes today.

THE QUEEN'S JUBILEE CELEBRATIONS

An item in the July magazine described the Jubilee celebrations as follows:

The day began with a quiet Eucharist at Streat. The bubbly activity started as people dropped off their food contributions at Westmeston Hall and proceeded up the road to St Martin's church. The west door was flung open wide. The sun poured in, bringing joy and anticipation to the congregation, most of whom were wearing red, white and blue. The Holy Spirit poured in a spirit of joy, warmth and enthusiasm. Never had Westmeston Church been so vibrantly full of the sound of music from musicians, choir and congregation or all ages. Canon John preached a great sermon of thankfulness to God for the Queen's fifty years of unstinting and dedicated service, underpinned by her strong faith. The National Anthem at the end of the service had an extra verse:

> *Not on this land alone*
> *But be God's mercies shown*
> *On every shore*
> *Lord, make the nations see*
> *That all humanity*
> *Should form one family*
> *The wide world over.*

The good fellowship which began in church lasted throughout the day as we all sat down to a sumptuous meal organised by Millie and her team. Tam and his barber shop quartet entertained us as we ate, and afterwards there were the games: shove halfpenny, darts, ball in the bucket, etc. The winners were awarded lollipops or Jubilee teddies. A jolly sing-song followed with Lyn at the keyboard, Matthew on the flute and a friend of Ian's on the drums, which was enjoyed by all. Tea and cakes followed, hardly needed after the huge lunch!

All went home tired but happy after a resounding successful day.

A huge thank you to all the helpers.

The magazine also contained eighteen photographs covering the events of the day, but unfortunately none are clear enough to include in this book.

NATIVITY CELEBRATIONS

Another wonderful event took place during the Christmas celebrations. Francis and Rosemond Baron (he was one-time chief executive of the RFU) lived in the largest and most impressive house in the hamlet – Streat Place. It was adjacent to the church and had its own pathway into the churchyard. The Barons were strong supporters of the stewardship scheme and Rosemond was confirmed during my incumbency. Streat Lane is unaltered almost from when it was first tarmacked and was so narrow that it had no markings. Streat Place boasted a wonderful driveway, which proved a Godsend whenever we held a special service, particularly weddings and funerals. The Barons very kindly opened up their gates on such occasions, so solving the parking problem.

Streat place was historically a farm, with lots of barns, most of which still lay to the back of the house. I had a vision of using some of them to re-enact the Bethlehem story and when I suggested my idea to the Barons, not only did they concur, but they volunteered to welcome all concerned into their magnificent baronial hall for mulled wine and mince pies afterwards. They also agreed to Lyn bringing her electric organ to accompany carol singing before the refreshments.

It was a cold evening, I remember, so a roaring fire set the atmosphere for a truly memorable evening.

The play began with Mary and Joseph emerging from one of the barns in the grounds of Streat Place that had been turned into their dwelling, and mounting a donkey to begin their journey to Bethlehem.

114

We followed, singing carols, as they moved round the side of the house, eventually stopping outside the front door of Streat Place, which was now the inn. Joseph advanced and knocked on the door. After a short while the door opened to reveal the innkeeper (Frances Baron), who said there was no room at the inn. He pointed, however, to a small outbuilding, which had been transformed into a stable, and told them that they could stay there if they wished. So the procession moved on to the stable and once they were safely in, I led the congregation in prayer. We then returned to the door of the inn where this time we were greeted and warmly invited in. Carol singing followed by refreshments ended a perfect occasion. The only problem was finding car parking, as one irate telephone call said that cars, way down the lane, were blocking the entrance to their house! It's an ill wind, however, because, as I have already recorded, the Barons thereafter opened up their drive when requested.

The evening was made perfect when I was given tickets by Francis to a rugby international at the famous stadium. See what I mean when I say, 'If the good Lord doesn't give, He sends!'? Needless to say, the event became an annual fixture, certainly until the three parishes were united upon my retirement.

Writing this reminds me of another kindness which enabled me to see Chelsea Football Club play at home. What's more, I was given extra tickets so that I could take my son and grandson as well! I have already mentioned that I visited every house at least twice in the two parishes during my time in office and this included non-church-attenders. It was from such a house that the tickets came. Additionally, church attendance was forthcoming. Not many clergy attempt house visiting on a grand scale, but I did and found it most rewarding both from the parish and my own point of view. It made people aware of the church's activities and indeed, many non-churchgoers became stalwart supporters of the social and fundraising activities in the parish. One such visit resulted in members of the family coming to special services, so I got to know them very well. What I didn't know at first was that they had strong connections with Chelsea, hence my tickets. The family also donated a wonderful oak chest (made from unwanted pews from the church), which housed items used at the children's church services. It also acted as two extra seats when needed. I sincerely hope that any of my fellow clergy who may read this will, if they don't already, include house visiting to their schedules from now on.

ONGOING MINISTRY

If I can jump forward a little, we stayed on in our house in Streat after retirement and witnessed Streat and Westmeston becoming the Beacon Parishes. But if I can also go back a bit, I must tell you how the rectory became our own. When I knew that after my retirement the three parishes were to be united under the one priest living in Ditchling, it became obvious that Streat Rectory would become surplus to diocesan requirements. I knew that after retirement, God willing, I would wish to continue being active and so it seemed logical to purchase the rectory so that we could stay on in Streat. Bishop Lindsay, having been made aware of my thoughts, kindly invited Millie and me to lunch to discuss the matter. I was delighted to hear that he supported my wishes. The archdeacon also agreed, so was set in motion the means to make this possible. I knew that the house would have to be valued independently, so three local housing agents submitted their valuations. The diocese agreed on the middle price, which we were happy to accept.

You may recall that we went to Streat on what is called 'a house for duty' agreement. I pointed out that by purchasing the vicarage I would lose some five years of free rates and other perks that came with being a priest for duty. I suggested that this might be taken into consideration when agreeing a price. I lost on that one, but what made my blood boil was when I was told that I would have to pay the diocesan legal fees as well as my own. I was told that it was normal practice when buying from the church. I exploded by saying, 'But I *am* the Church, full-time since 1952!' I also pointed out that due to moving from the church in Wales to England, my pension fund was frozen for about five years as, at that time, there was no reciprocal agreement between the two churches. My pension, therefore, was about £1,000 a year less that it would have been. I was told to fight this, but replied, 'I joined the Church to serve it, not to fight it.' But being asked now to pay the diocesan legal expenses was the last straw. I dug my heels in and finally, after protracted argument, won the day.

St George's Retreat and
St John The Evangelist

St George's Retreat, situated between Burgess Hill and Haywards Heath, comes within the Beacon Parish boundaries and that is where we moved when finally leaving Streat. Before moving on, however, I need first to share with you a little of its history, especially as I became more and more involved in its ministry. David Wallis, the vicar of the new combined parish, was constantly being asked by Sister Mary Thomas to provide some form of Anglican ministry. He asked me if I would take it on and I agreed. A brief summary will better set the scene.

The congregation of 'The sisters of St Augustine of the Mercy of Jesus' was served by the Reverend John Maes at Bruges, Belgium. As his ministry progressed, he became increasingly concerned regarding the welfare of individuals suffering from mental illness, whose hospital was within his parish in Bruges. He became convinced that the then-current methods of supervision of patients was obsolete, overly severe and lacking in any genuine loving care. In such conditions he felt that the spiritual influence of the sisters would be invaluable and with the agreement of nineteen young sisters, he founded the above order. He was later appointed by the bishop to take over the direction of St Julian's Mental Institution in Bruges and immediately set about introducing the sisters to take responsibility for the patients' care. He insisted that his foundations should be called 'God's Hotels'.

During the nineteenth century, a number of new religious orders were founded within the Roman Catholic Church on the continent, devoted wholly to undertaking missionary work in England. So it came to pass that Father John Maes arrived in Westbury. He later assisted his brother in setting up the society's foundation. In 1864, the Purchase Estate of 251 acres, located to the north of Ditchling Common, was put up for sale, including the mansion house and its contents, and Purchase Farm, together with its farm buildings and machinery. The society bought it. Two years later, Canon Maes arrived in Sussex accompanied by three Augustinian nuns and took up residence in the mansion, which they renamed St Mary's. Soon afterwards, parties of Belgium craftsmen and workmen arrived to build the new institution. Not only were the men brought from Belgium, but the building materials as well, which didn't go down well with the Ditchling residents. St George's was opened in 1868, with space for 150 patients. The work flourished, so much so that today there are nineteen establishments throughout the United Kingdom. At St George's alone there is now accommodation for 180 patients. During the course of my ministry, I have visited similar homes all over the world, but none of them come anywhere near to the loving care offered to its residents at St George's.

The privileged ministry I exercise at St George's is as rewarding as any I have undertaken anywhere. But more of that later; I must now return to Streat and Westmeston.

A MAN WITH A MISSION

I started writing my biography in 2000 and finished it in 2009. Why so long? The answer is easy; I always put people before things. But having said that, I must admit that, like most things, one has to be in the mood for writing. And there is something else; both books are written entirely from memory, which explains any chronological errors, and it was only from time to time that a flash back to a previous incident prompted me to pick up my pen and write or, to be more accurate, to sit before my computer and attempt to get it down. It wasn't until I went to Warnham that I entered the complicated arena of computers and without the help of good friends that came to my rescue, the book would never have been finished. Even then there were calamities I had to struggle with such as when I pressed the wrong button and lost the first fifty pages. It took a great deal of will power to start again; indeed, it is only because of the encouragement of loved ones (plus a text from the bible talking about having put your hands to the plough) that I soldiered on.

Today, sitting at my computer, I am amazed that I am now well into my second book, which begins where I left off the first, leaving Thailand after the death of my dear wife Rose. I still put people before things, but being so-called 'retired', I now have more spare time. And although I still need the help of friends from time to time, I have obviously improved my knowledge of computers. Indeed, I now regard mine as a friend not, as when I started, an enemy! I passed a milestone today in that I reached page 100. This means I am about three quarters of the way to completion and should finish it within two years from start to finish.

It was from Streat then that *A Man with a Mission* was printed. I found a publisher, The Book Guild, whose offices were in Brighton and I enjoyed very much following the progress of its printing and eventual publication. I remember the thrill of holding the first copy in my hands, also of addressing groups about its contents. I was advised that if I really wanted to gain wide publication I should find an agent, but as I said in its foreword, I just wanted to show God's blessing on my ministry, a ministry which was even now ongoing. And I didn't want selling books to get in the way of it. One thousand copies were printed and I still have about forty left. The publishers priced it at £17.99, which Amazon reduced immediately. The rewards have not been in finance, but in the knowledge that many who have read it see the hand of God through its pages. I can ask for nothing more.

A book signing for *A Man With a Mission* at the golf club.

THE REMEMBRANCE GARDEN AT STREAT

In the autumn of 2005, the parish went through a very painful time when three of its younger daughters died, all within a very short time of each other. They were all very gifted in their own ways. Furthermore, they were all very young, much too young to die. They all came from leading church families, so their deaths affected the whole parish; with it came a desire to remember them in some specific way. Their names were Jane Hill, Lucy Yeldham and Rebecca Skelton. It occurred to me that a suitable memorial could be a garden of remembrance. Attached to the original vicarage was a sizable barn; when the diocese sold the vicarage, they retained the barn and have been renting it out to the parish for a peppercorn rent ever since. I encouraged the parish to buy it, thereby having some of our assets in property. This came to pass and the barn continued to be used for meetings, social occasions and it was hired out for a small rent to local villagers. To one side of the

The garden of remembrance.

120

barn was a plot of land, which belonged to the then-owner of the old vicarage, Mrs Colt. She was an American lady (a part of the Colt Revolver family) who spent six months exactly in the UK and the other half of the year in the states. I asked her if she would donate the plot of land in question and she agreed. So was born the remembrance garden.

It was previously used only for rubbish and bonfires, so the transformation to a beautiful garden was amazing. When the idea surfaced, I let it be known publically, hoping that donations would come in to make the transformation possible; I was not disappointed. In fact donations covered all expenses, including the plants to go in the garden. Fiona Smith, a well-known landscape gardener, planned and executed its transformation, and we opened up a side door of the barn, giving access to the garden, and so was created a great asset to the parish and a garden of remembrance also. In addition to the garden, Jane's family donated a wonderful eight-branched, wrought-iron candelabrum, wall-mounted for Streat Church; Rebecca's family designed and made a bird bath monument with the initials of the ladies inscribed on it, housed in the garden; Lucy's parents created a lovely stone seat for use near her grave, which has been gratefully used by visitors ever since.

As I have already said, all three made important contributions during their young lives. Lucy was incredibly brave in the face of a long illness. The depth of love and affection by those present at Rebecca's funeral was a living testimony to her nature. But, as Jane alone lived in the parish, I want to share with you what an exceptional person she was. She suffered with cancer, but never complained. A priest is supposed to bring comfort and solace when visiting, but the opposite was true when I visited Jane. I always left receiving far more than I had given. She was so cheerful, upbeat and generous. I never left without a jar of homemade jam or the like. Her courage was infectious, all of this coming from a deep Christian faith. Despite her illness, she always brought her children to church and was like a ray of sunshine as she entered. When she was too sick to make the journey, I used to take sick communion at her home. One of my last visits was on a lovely sunny day, so I suggested that we held the service in the garden. She happily agreed but first shut her dog in the house, for the sake of peace and quiet. I had reached the moment of consecrating the elements when a visitor entered the house and immediately let the dog out into the garden. Quick as a flash, he bounded down to where we were and swept the consecrated bread into his mouth with his tail wagging like mad. For a second we both sat transfixed then simultaneously burst out into riotous laughter! I quickly consecrated some more bread and the service came to an end without further mishap. Jane proudly proclaimed to one and all that she had the holiest dog in the parish!

Brave Jane rises to the challenge

Report: Charlotte Taylor
charlotte.taylor@jpress.co.uk

JELLY babies, chocolate and sheer guts gave cancer sufferer Jane Hill the edge to pull off the London to Brighton bike ride.

Jane, 44, has been battling breast cancer for three years and took on the incredible challenge to raise cash for her local church.

Her husband Andrew was at her side throughout the ride and talked her through it.

She said: "It was mind over matter.

"We took it very slowly with lots of chocolate and jelly babies and plenty of breaks and it was great fun."

Even the formidable hulk of Ditchling Beacon at the end of the ride failed to faze her.

"I cycled up Ditchling Beacon and I felt like the king of the world. My husband was beside me and kept saying 'I know you can do it'."

What makes Jane's achievement even more remarkable is that she did not do any training.

"I have a dog and I exercise her for an hour every day and therefore myself. That keeps me basically fit and I swim.

"I wasn't fit enough but I had decided in my mind I was going to do it. I'm very strong minded."

Jane, who is currently undergoing treatment, lives in Ditchling with her husband and children aged six and four.

Her heroic efforts have raised more than £550 for Streat Church.

She is a member of the church and is grateful for all their support over the last three years.

"They have been a great source of strength and they are a wonderful bunch of people."

STRONG MINDED: Jane Hill

Canon John said the cash would go towards rewiring the church.

He said: "She is an incredible and brave person."

Brave Jane Hill.

Before sickness took its toll, Jane was a nursing sister. Although no longer active in this field, the qualities of her profession remained. She knew that I was undergoing treatment for my prostate cancer and despite her failing health, never ceased to enquire after mine. She also knew that I was having problems sleeping at night and bombarded me with herbal medicines, homemade jams, but above all with love and concern. Whatever I took, be it communion or a special cross to be held in one's hand, she always gave more than she received. She let it be known that her funeral was to be upbeat and in keeping with her wishes, it was. Her best friend wore a bright pink dress! Her journey from church to graveside was in a magnificent horse-drawn carriage that turned every head as it went by. Inevitably, if I am at a funeral, it is because I am conducting it. This was one funeral where I wished to be in the congregation, just one amongst the fellow mourners, sharing in their grief.

One of the highlights of the year was the London to Brighton bicycle race that passed through Ditchling, where Jane lived. Despite her advancing cancer, she insisted on taking part, as a copy of the West Sussex Times newspaper article proves. I have met some incredible people in my lifetime, but for all round qualities, Jane takes the top prize. What particularly thrilled me was the depth of her faith, which shone through in everything she did. She is one of the people that I am looking forward to seeing most when at the end of my pilgrimage I too (hopefully) make that journey to Revelations 21 verses 1–7.

OUTDOOR SERVICE AT THE GALLOPS

One of the highlights of the parish year was undoubtedly the outdoor service held in the grounds of Barry and Helen Firman's house. Streat Place and the Gallops were the two largest houses in the hamlets and it is an indication of the community spirit in the parish that both houses were involved in its life. Apart from the service, Barry and Helen also hosted an outdoor concert run by artists from Glyndebourne. The size and beauty of the Gallops garden proved to be the perfect setting for such an occasion. Both events were huge successes. I was thrilled when visiting Bishop Lindsay's office to see a large photo of the service hanging on the most prominent place in his study.

The service had as its centrepiece a large cross made up like a jigsaw puzzle, which, when slotted together, revealed the following message:

**GOD
has
reconciled
all things to himself
through the death of
JESUS
on the
cross**

There were about fifteen pieces that together made up the words above, each piece being carried by a representative of one of the groups or officers of the parish, accompanied by a flag-bearer naming the activity of the carrier. I was so overjoyed as I watched the procession carrying its contributions, advancing to the cross, that I cried. That procession revealed the extent of the activities and depth of the community participation in the ministry of the church. There was clapping from the large congregation as Bishop Lindsay placed the last piece into

Bishop Lindsay completes the jigsaw.

124

place. The morning was rounded off by everyone enjoying a picnic in the lovely grounds of the house. I was particularly pleased to see how Bishop Lindsay moved among the people, sharing in their food and drink – the bishop among his flock, fulfilling his role perfectly as our Father in God.

Our hosts at the Gallops.

You may recall that at the beginning of my time at Streat and Westmeston I set out a plan of action, including to prepare the parish to become an equal partner with Ditchling when the three parishes became one. As the time for my retirement drew neater, I was able to look back with some satisfaction. Both churches had been put in a good state of repair. The following photo shows Paul Charmin and myself inspecting the repairs to the roof of St Martin's.

Thanks to successful and continued stewardship, the finances were in excellent condition, meeting all demands placed upon them. There was also an excellent relationship between the two hamlets. This meant that when the merger came we could hold our heads up high, which we did.

Paul Charmin inspects St Martin's roof.

Inevitably the time drew ever nearer for me to hang up my boots. I wanted to try and leave on a high and hit on the idea of an auction. With the expected numbers to the auction on the Saturday and my farewell service on the Sunday, there was nowhere large enough to accommodate the anticipated congregations. We knew of a large marquee at Plumpton Race Course, which we were able to hire for the weekend. The auction was a great success and raised more than enough money to cover all costs, with funds left over for the parish as well. As for the service, I can only say it was inspirational. There were various items in the service which I will long treasure, including an African choir and twelve young people from the parish giving a recital on the drums. Bishop Lindsay preached and as usual, was inspiring. During the refreshments after the service, my children, Mike and Elizabeth, startled me by presenting a 'This Is Your Life' complete with slides. As I watched the presentation I had to pinch myself. Was that really

Chui from Hong Kong.

all about me? That weekend I will never forget, with grateful thanks to all those who made it so special. What made it even more special was when a letter was read out by my daughter, Elizabeth, from Chui Kwork Hun, a Chinese friend from my days in Hong Kong. To my amazement, she then said that he was not satisfied with writing a letter; he had, for the first time in his life, left Hong Kong to be with me! Sure enough sitting in the congregation was Chui, who rose to his feet as I approached and we embraced. We had corresponded with each other regularly for the last fifty years, but never in my wildest dreams could I have imagined such a reunion. Very sadly he died shortly after returning to the colony. In *A Man with a Mission* I described how he nearly became a Christian. I believe that through the grace of God he, together with Jane Hill, will greet me when I too make that journey to our eternal home.

Everyone knew that when Streat, Westmeston and Ditchling became united under the banner of the Beacon Parishes there would be many changes. It was of course the main reason for our purchasing Streat Rectory, so that I could continue helping in the extended parish. Against this, however, there is a strong tradition that a retiring priest should move on, leaving the coast clear for the new incumbent. I faced the

127

<u>A Thank you to Canon John</u>

Dear Canon John we'd like to say
A great big thanks to you today!

You made our children's church such fun
You taught us all about God's son

You helped us laugh and sing and pray
We're going to miss you from today

But we understand that you need a rest
And we promise you that we'll do our best

To carry on our songs and praise
the way you've taught us to
And so to end we'd like to say **God Bless You!**

Children's Church, Streat
Sunday 28th January 2007

The children's farewell.

same dilemma when I moved to Warnham as my predecessor moved back into the village due to the kindness of the Lucas family, who loaned him one of their houses. He took no services in the church, unless by my invitation, and on the whole everything worked out well. The situation in the Beacon Parish, however, was very different as there was now one priest covering three churches, so he needed help. In addition there was the ministry at St George's, which I had taken on at the vicar's request and which he certainly wanted me to continue. I also helped out in the parish when requested. If the truth be known, however, I was not spiritually at peace. Rightly or wrongly, I sensed tension in my relationships with others and reluctantly came to the conclusion that we should move on. Streat vicarage had, thanks to Millie, a beautifully kept garden, but it was now sadly proving too much for her, so the question of moving was given an added impulse.

Whilst talking of gardens, incidentally, it would be extremely remiss of me not to mention the flower festivals held in both churches. The festivals were always based on a spiritual theme, the result being both beautiful and inspirational. In addition to the festivals, the churches were also decorated on special occasions, such as Harvest, Easter and

Dear John

Sorry I can't be with you tonight but it is a great pleasure to
be able to contribute. I have known John since the mid
sixties. Practical common sense and concern for people are a
hallmark of his ministry. His ministry among seafarers was
outstanding. He built the Mission in Dar-es- Salaam into
what was, and still is, amongst the finest anywhere in the
world. He related easily and naturally with people of all
levels, as at home with a ship's captain as a cabin boy, He
became a close friend of Tanzania's president Julius Nyere,
and Ambassadors of many nationalities, Archbishops, clergy
and with many of those with whom he came in contact.
If I had to sum up his gifts I would say:-
-      He is a man of vision, enthusiasm, energy, and
exceptional ability
-      He is cheerful and open with everyone, transparently
good
-      He has courage, determination, a love of people, deep
joy of living and a lovely sense of humour
-      He is a born leader, loyal friend and exceptional
fundraiser

Most important of all he is:A man of God, a faithful priest,
and a man who knows what he believes and who practices
what he preaches

Like us all, he is human and does have some faults and
failings. He likes his own way, it's difficult to get a word in
edgeways when he is in free flow, and he has tunnel vision
when he sees something that needs to be done.

John, all of us love you for what you are, for what you have
done, for what you mean to us, and for the wonderful priest
and friend you are.

'Well done, good and faithful servant'.

Bishop Down's letter read at my farewell service.

Christmas. Great credit in this should go to Paul Charmin, who spared
no effort in producing stunning results.

ST JOHN THE EVANGELIST, BURGESS HILL

Coinciding with our move to St George's, the parish of St John's
entered an interregnum. I only knew the church at all because of a
confirmation service held a few years ago, at which six of my people
from Streat and Westmeston were confirmed. When I received a call
from a Bernie Widdowson, asking me if I could help out during the
interregnum, I immediately agreed. Why? I have received many such
calls during my ministry, but none as sincere and appealing as his.

So began a relationship with the church and members of the

congregation that grew stronger with every service I attended. Not only did I find the services rewarding but was overwhelmed with the welcome and kindnesses I received from the congregation. Once the interregnum was over, I enjoyed just being a member of the congregation, although I still robed and assisted in the distribution of the elements and also took other services when called upon. The new vicar, Kevin O'Brien, impressed me with his vision of what St John's should be, and involved me as little or as much as I felt able to contribute. He also offered me his friendship, which I gratefully accepted. It was a wrench leaving the Beacon Parishes, but at St John's I found friendship and a growth in spirituality, which more than compensated for our loss. In time, Bernie handed over the mantle of head server to Colin Squires, who was (and still is) church warden. Both Bernie and Colin are blessed with their wives, Kit and Jill. Father Kevin also has the devoted support of his wife, Sue, and Lay Reader Linda Blaker. I could go on listing the names of devoted servants of the Lord, but hope I have said enough to paint a picture of a thriving and loving church, motivated by the faith of devoted Christians. One parishioner (Friar Tuck as she is happily known) constantly embarrasses me with gifts of cakes and jams. Embarrassed or not, Ruth, please keep it up!

You may recall that when I was at Warnham I had a dream of the parish being the social as well as the spiritual heart of the village. I admire St John's for going a long way towards achieving that aim. In addition to its services during the week and on Sundays, it uses its parish room and church to host the community food bank and the stroke club, as well as providing a credit union drop-in; hosting a mental health drop-in, and mums and toddlers groups; providing cookery classes for those in sheltered accommodation; providing low-cost lunches and work experience in the Spire Café; hosting an evening concert each month and regularly hosting civic receptions, charity events, services and charity concerts; hosting exhibitions for local schools and charity groups for art, photography, etc. Additionally, a wildflower and wildlife conservation area has just been created in the churchyard.

The maintenance of church property is always a challenge and St John's is no exception. Sadly the heating system at St John's has just broken down beyond repair and the only option now is total replacement. The recent survey of the church and its heating needs has projected an estimated cost of £100,000, including VAT. And that is the most cost-efficient option!

Throughout my ministry I have constantly been involved in fundraising

130

schemes. Praise the Lord, this is not now my responsibility! Although, as members of the congregation, we have of course responded to the appeal.

THE RETIREMENT VILLAGE

My ministry at St George's started whilst still at Streat and was still ongoing at the time of moving, so it seemed a natural step to move into the retirement village, and that's exactly what we did in 2012. The sale of the rectory covered all expenses in purchasing and moving, as well as adding useful touches to the flat. We were very sad to leave Streat and so many dear friends, but once we were settled into St George's we knew we had done the right thing, and have been extremely happy ever since. Because St George's is only a mile from my last parish, we are able to maintain contact with old friends. This is made so obvious when from time to time I take services in my old parish and enjoy meeting up with old acquaintances.

Some explanation is now needed about the retirement village, situated in the grounds of St George's Park and owned by the Augustine nuns. The original convent also housed wards (although the word is not allowed; rather they were called homes) for the sick. As the years advanced, however, the facilities failed to comply with NHS standards. The nuns were told that the work would have to be closed down. They, however, had other ideas. They decided to build three new care homes in the grounds, which would be paid for by building and selling flats also in the grounds. So was born the retirement village. To own an apartment one had to be fifty-nine or over, but one of the joys is to see children and grandchildren visiting their beloved parents and grandparents. With us it includes visits from great grandchildren as well!

The last stage of the final block of flats is even now being constructed, together with a social centre, complete with a swimming pool. Along with the other residents, we have access to the gym, the library, the games room, a hairdressing salon, a chiropodist and masseur, and an excellent restaurant. To complete the facilities, there is also a shop. The staff are exceptional, nothing is too much bother for them, and they couldn't be kinder. I give but one instance: there was a fairly new resident who came regularly to the restaurant, but suddenly stopped. He was ninety-six, incidentally. Sarah, who had been serving him at his table, was so concerned that she, together with a colleague, went to his apartment to check that he was all right. He was, but was most grateful for her concern. How do I know? Because he told me.

Apart from the swimming pool, all of these facilities are housed in Maes Court (see photograph below). We also boast a bowling green and croquet lawn. Don't ask me how, but somehow I find myself in the croquet team!

Apart from the facilities mentioned, the residents have set up various activity groups, which just goes to show the enthusiasm and the versatility of the residents. Depending on your wishes, there are groups for line dancing, bowls (both indoor and outdoor), balance, snooker, short tennis, table tennis, walking, mahjong (puzzle), drawing and painting, cribbage, scrabble, knitting and nattering, armchair yoga, a quiz and of course Catholic and Anglican services. A very successful choir has also been formed and together with other entertainers, gives concerts in the concert hall. Lectures on topical themes are also held on a regular basis.

Such a wide choice of activities says a great deal about the residents themselves, a large number of which reached the top of the tree in their

Maes Court.

chosen profession. Our present chairman of the Residents' Association for example, Her Honour Judge Shirley Anwyl QC, was called to the bar by the Inner Temple, practised as a junior barrister and took silk (became Queen's Council) in 1979. In 1995 she was appointed Circuit Judge-Resident (Senior) Judge of Woolwich Crown Court. Her work in the law for forty-four years is now put to good use as our chairperson.

Amongst the residents there are three professors, three doctors, two clergymen, two knights and their ladies, two or three head teachers, a Baroness and a number of very highly decorated servicemen. Nearly every resident has been successful in their own right and has an interesting story to tell.

I have written elsewhere of the Missions to Seamen providing a home from home through their clubs and missions. The retirement village provides the same service, with the added bonus that the residents themselves are willing to share their expertise for the benefit of all. There are good Samaritans who freely give advice or practical help on computers, television or gardening, for example, infusing their expertise to running the various activities for the benefit of the residents.

Old age inevitably brings health problems of one sort or another. It is inspirational to witness how those affected cope with their disabilities and make the best of any given situation. Some residents are in their nineties, yet manage to cope admirably and without any complaint. It is a real privilege to know them. I could write something interesting about nearly all of them but will limit my list to three.

Norman Watson, who is probably the youngest resident in the village, aged sixty-four, was the victim of a stroke in 1964 that has left him paralysed down one half of his body and with impaired speech. He spends most of his days in a wheelchair and has a full-time carer. However, whenever he arrives at the restaurant, he seems to light up the room with his winning smile. He carries a little notebook with him, which he uses to great effect. Folk coming in and out invariably stop at his table to pass the day with him and in the case of the ladies, he usually gets a kiss as well. I tease him that he gets more kisses than I do!

He expressed great interest in my book, which, needless to say, won him a copy. A very kind neighbour used to read him a passage from it most evenings, until it was finished. He frequently asks me when he can have the next instalment.

He recently took part in a mammoth swimming distance challenge to raise funds for one of his favourite charities. Needless to say, he completed the distance and made a lot of money.

Catherine John is an elderly resident who is blind. This does not stop her from attending the restaurant every day, where her Scottish accent can be heard amid all the other voices around her table. She has her favourite spot in the entrance to Maes Court where she sits, and again very few pass by without stopping to have a chat or pass the time of day with her. Being Scottish she is not averse to a night cap, although when in our flat after supper one night, she asked for a brandy rather than a whisky!

Wherever we go, we seem blessed with kindnesses beyond the call of duty and St George's is no exception. To find dear friends when well into one's eighties is a real blessing and we have been well blessed.

I have mentioned elsewhere how one partner lovingly looks after the other, and nowhere is this more apparent than with Leslie and Doreen Pointer, aged ninety-two and a half, Leslie proudly told me! They both walk with the aid of a stick, one holding tight to the other. Whenever I see them I am reminded of the Pied Piper, with the children following on behind. They usually come for lunch, but arrive about half an hour before lunch is due. Why? Because Leslie never misses his daily trip to the gym where he works out for half an hour. Doreen waits patiently in the foyer until he appears then off they go for a well-earned lunch.

Almost without exception, the residents feel privileged to be here and show it by playing their part in making it a Garden of Eden. As for me, I have spent a lifetime trying to create such a haven for those I have served, so feel I am now receiving my just reward!

There must surely be some disadvantage, you may ask. Well, there is. One makes friends very easily and quickly, but because we are an aging community, one can lose friends as quickly as one makes them.

Because I began my ministry at St George's while still at Streat, I visited the care homes when they were all housed in the convent. I witnessed the new buildings being erected and the patients being moved to their new homes. I was so impressed by the way the move took place, which, as far as I could see, went without a hitch.

Because a good number of the residents from St Mary's care home came from the Wivelsfield, the neighbouring parish, its Vicar looks after the Anglicans there. I also visit St Mary's on occasions, when the need arises. The other two wards, St Rita's and St Clare's, are my babies and servicing them is as rewarding as any other activity I have undertaken during my fifty-five years as a priest. To keep the service as simple as possible, I conduct the communion services without the use of a book, the same with the Bible. I take every part of it by heart. Every patient receives communion or a blessing and I have a little chat with them (with the exception, of course, of those who are asleep!) before giving them the Blessed Sacrament.

THE MOVE TO ST GEORGE'S

Whilst still at Streat, we witnessed the building of the latest block of flats in the village named 'The Cedars'. One of which we decided (No. 11) was to be our new home. Apart from anything else, we had breath-taking views from our windows. Alas, we were told that there were already eight clients before us and advised to choose another flat, but we were adamant that it was to number 11 that we would move. Unbelievably, one by one, the potential clients dropped out, until the day came when we were told that, if we still wanted it, it could be ours.

Because we had booked it before it was finished, we were given the choice of certain fittings, which was an added inducement. Trust the Taylors, but number 11 was one of the most expensive on the block! But, as already explained, the sale of the rectory allowed us to cover all expenses. So it came to pass that during holy week 2012, we moved into our new home.

Moving is an absorbing business, so much so that it caused me to forget an extremely important occasion; on the Friday I had nipped across to the shop in Maes Court and bumped into a resident, Mary Royall, who was to become, with her husband Peter, a good friend. She noticed my dog collar and remarked that she was surprised to see me here and not in church. When I enquired why, she said, 'Because it's Good Friday.' I had become so engrossed in the move that I had completely forgotten the day!

I had not been in residence very long before I noticed that ministry was needed for Anglicans within the village itself. An approach to Sister Mary Thomas produced positive results. Space for my robes was made in the vestry cupboards, but even more importantly, space at the altar so that I could celebrate Holy Communion in St George's Catholic church. Possibly even more important was the way I was accepted as part of the overall ministry of St George's – altogether a very humbling experience.

We have now been here for three years, during which time a lot of water has flowed under the bridge: friends have been and gone; no less than six residents have been transferred from the village to one of the care homes, where of course I continue to see them in my monthly services at St Clare's and St Rita's; I also hold two services a month in St George's Church and at present have a monthly Bible class for about twelve residents. I recently calculated that I have ministered communion to a thousand souls since I started my ministry here. Father Rick, the Roman Priest who serves the nuns from his church in Burgess Hill, is kindness itself. In addition to the services, I am frequently called upon to administer the last rites, to visit the sick, including house communions when required, and of course to conduct funerals. I have been given to understand that at least half of the residents from the care homes are Anglican, so by the grace of Almighty God, there is a real ministry to fulfil in the village and in the homes.

Once the remaining block of flats is completed, there will be about 320 people in the village. Millie and I are one of the few couples who walk unaided, which means that there is an abundance of walking sticks, Zimmers, push chairs and motorised buggies constantly on the move. These aids to movement definitely slow things down; indeed, I can say with complete confidence that the speed (or lack of it) reveals one's age. The other giveaway is rising from one's chair. The struggle to stand upright and the effort required to do so immediately reveal age. I know this from my own efforts to move around! But it is inspiring is to see how one partner supports the other. In marriage the couple promise to love, honour and obey each other, in sickness and in health, till death do them part. Most couples are young when they make these vows and unable to really appreciate what lies ahead. However, as to the manner born, they embrace the challenge when it comes. My dear brother Peter is a shining example of this. Thelma, his wife, has dementia and needs help in the smallest of things. When I questioned him, he said, 'For around seventy years she looked after me, and if the situation was reversed would do exactly the same for me. Now it's my turn.'

I know that being a carer in such circumstances is extremely demanding and if the truth be known, there is a similarity for me in my ministry here. It is common knowledge that as one gets older everything demands more and more effort. But what is also true is that if one makes the effort the reward is well worthwhile. This can be particularly true when taking services in the care homes. In a parish, one is used to babies crying and children making a noise (Suffer the little children to come unto me!) and if the worst comes to the worst a parent will usually come to the rescue. There is no such escape route in the homes. At any one time someone will stand up and move around, others may indulge in a conversation with someone who is not there, yet others sleep peacefully, so one has to make a decision about whether or not to wake them up to give them communion. A patient who is normally meek and friendly can without warning become aggressive, so one has to be aware of any eventuality. I take the service without the aid of a prayer book, which makes it easier if there is an interruption. Nevertheless, I am privileged to say that, as I near the end of my ministry, I have never felt more fulfilled in doing the Lord's work than now. After I have given everyone present their communion or a blessing, I say, 'How better can we say thank you than by saying together the Lord's Prayer.' So I begin by reciting out loud, 'Our Father.' Often, as I begin the prayer, I am almost a lone voice (crying the wilderness?) But as I progress more and more into the prayer so others join in. It is as if the Lord's Prayer unlocks doors, reawakens memories long forgotten. So much so that the prayer ends in a crescendo of praise, joy and thanksgiving. 'Praise the Lord!' Inevitably there are some who can't attend because of failing health, so once the service is over I visit their rooms to give them a blessing and in some cases, communion for the sick. I am deeply moved when recognised. To see their faces light up with a beautiful smile is the most rewarding gift that I could possibly receive.

I am amazed at the love and affection shown by all the staff to the patients, especially after hearing of abuse in other homes in the country. As for me, I get cuddles and occasionally kisses too. Recently I went into the room of one of the residents who is well into her nineties. On the wall was a large notice that read, 'Okay, I'm up for a toy boy as long as he's got his own teeth!'

To give further examples, a few days after moving in, when one still couldn't move for unopened boxes, and nothing seemed to work, enquiries about how we were settling in came from Craig as he served our meal in the restaurant. After explaining my woes he volunteered to help. 'I'm not very good at fixing things,' he said, 'but I am happy to give it a go!' He did and with such success that in no time at all the television was working, and I was able to deal with all the emails that had piled up on my computer. When I offered to repay him for his kindness, he firmly refused to accept anything. 'You spend your life helping others,' he said, 'so it is an honour to do something for you.'

On another occasion, I was visiting a lady in her room and after some conversation, I asked her, 'Would you like me to give you a blessing?'

'Oh yes, please,' she replied. 'I'd love a cup of tea!'

On a very recent occasion, I was taking a communion service for about twenty-five souls in the congregation. Having said my morning prayers before going to the home, I was struck by the lesson (one of my favourites), 'The Prodigal Son'. So in my address before the communion, I told them the story. I came to a delightful gentleman, who had been very quiet up to this moment and was about to give him his communion when he burst out, 'I am the prodigal son! I have been naughty but I am back home again now!'

Conclusion

Looking back at my ministry, I can see a golden thread that has helped me on every stage of my pilgrimage through life and that is (so they tell me) my warm and friendly smile. Times without number, people have told me how they love it. However, looking back at my life, something I have had to cope with which has given me the most aggravation is my protruding teeth. Unfortunately, possibly because of the Second World War years, nothing was done to straighten them out as a child, so for eighty-five years I have had to endure protruding teeth. I still remember receiving a letter from a pen friend when we were both about ten years old. She wrote, 'I do hope your old fangs don't still hang out!'

Even worse, whilst I was a lay reader in the mission at London Docks, a priest said to me, 'You could never be a priest with those teeth in the pulpit!'

Today I have lost most of my teeth, except for the two at the front! St Paul spoke of having a cross to bear regarding his person; well, I've had mine. Yet when I think about it, those teeth have been part of my smile which through the grace of Almighty God has helped me immensely in my ministry. It is the perfect example of one's weakness being transformed into his strength.

We are all as God made us and provided we use our gifts (or the lack of them) in his service, we need fear nothing.

However, our gifts cannot solve all problems, especially those that come with old age. 'The spirit is willing, but the flesh is weak.' So, for example, in taking a service, one comes to a part which is known by heart, yet the mind suddenly becomes blank. This is happening more and more to me. As for climbing steps and arising from one's seat, what was once achieved without even thinking now becomes a challenge! At least at St George's one is in good company! But yet again, man's weakness brings forth grace in seeing how one partner cares and supports the other. I am deeply moved by what I see, for such dedication to another turns hardship into a deep and lasting joy.

As for me, I am constantly being told by others that I must now learn to say NO, but I reply that priesthood is a vocation, which can't be turned off like a tap when things get difficult or when you reach a certain age. Marriage, however, is also a vocation, for better or for worse, for richer or for poorer, in sickness and in health, until death do us part. The obligation to maintain that vocation becomes more challenging with advancing age and increasing fragility.

Many say that I will know when the time comes for me to hang up my boots. As recorded in *A Man with a Mission*, despite my father being an atheist who did his best to put me off church activity, the hand of God was far more powerful, drew me irresistibly towards Him and has kept me in His care ever since. I hesitate to say that God is speaking to me directly now, but I must admit that there are signs certainly telling me to ease off before closing down altogether. I remember a wise Father in God telling me when I retired at seventy that I would now have more time for prayer and he was right. I have now retired three and a half times and the desire and ability to pray has remained. I know it will continue no matter how many times I attempt to retire, for my vocation demands it.

What I do know is that there will not be a third volume of autobiography, so this is it. So in closing and saying goodbye I want to record my deepest thanks to all those who have journeyed with me during my pilgrimage of life, to say sorry to any I have treated unfairly and to ask you to pray for me as I do for you.

God bless,
John

William begins his Christian pilgrimage as my ministry draws to a close.